Jazz Piano Vocabulary

Volume 5
The Mixolydian Scale

by Roberta Piket

With additional material available
on-line at www.muse-eek.com

Muse Eek Publishing Company
New York, New York

Copyright © 2003 by Roberta Piket. All rights reserved

ISBN 1594899584

No part of this publication may be reproduced, stored in a
retrieval system, or transmitted, in any form or by any means,
electronic, mechanical, photocopying, recording, or otherwise,
without the prior written permission of the publisher.

Printed in the United States

This publication can be purchased from your local bookstore or by contacting:
Muse Eek Publishing Company
P.O. Box 509
New York, NY 10276, USA
Phone: 212-473-7030
Fax: 212-473-4601
http://www.muse-eek.com
sales@muse-eek.com

Table Of Contents

Acknowledgements	iv
About the Author	v
Foreword	vi
How to Use This Book	vii
Swung Eighth Notes	viii
Order Of Presentation	viii
Fingering	ix
Introduction To The Mixolydian Mode	10
Applying The Mixolydan Mode To Improvisation	12
Dominant Seventh Chord Tones	12
Dominant Seventh Chord Tensions	12
Suspended Chord Tones	13
Suspended Chord Tensions	14
Explanation of Left Hand Chord Voicings	15
Dominant Seventh Voicings	15
Dominant Seventh Sus Voicings	16
The Dominant Seventh Sus Chord as a Passing Chord	16
Mixolydian Modes: Fingerings And Left Hand Chord Voicings	18
Hand Position	18
Practice Method	18
Dynamics	19
Using The Left Hand Chord Voicings	19
Swung Eight Notes, Articulation and Phrasing	19
The Modes	20
Examples of Melodic Lines Using the Mixolydian Mode	23
Dominant Seventh Chord Ideas	23
Dominant Seventh Sus Chord Ideas	25
Your Ideas	26
An Introduction To Approach Notes	28
The Blues	35
The Blues Scale	35
Basic Blues Form	36
Keeping The Form	36
Listening To The Blues	36
Mixin' It Up: A Mixolydian Etude On The Blues	38
Further Exploration	41
Supplemental Cross-Sectional Jazz Piano Discography	41
What Next?	43

Acknowledgments

The author gratefully acknowledges Bruce Arnold for his invaluable feedback and Muse Eek Publishing for the opportunity to publish this book.

Thanks to Mike Garson for permission to use his beautiful artwork.

Special thanks to Billy Mintz for research assistance and encouragement.

About the Author

Roberta Piket is from Queens, NY. Her father, composer Frederick Piket, gave her her first piano lessons when she was seven years old. Roberta began playing seriously in her early teens, studying jazz piano with Walter Bishop, Jr and classical piano with Vera Wels. After graduating from prestigious Hunter College High School, she entered the joint double-degree program at Tufts University and the New England Conservatory of Music, earning a Bachelor's Degree in Computer Science from the former and a Bachelor's Degree in Jazz Studies from the latter. During this time she studied privately with Fred Hersch, Stanley Cowell, Jim McNeely and Bob Moses. Soon after graduation Roberta returned to New York City to devote herself to music full-time, which she has done ever since. In New York, she studied for six years with Richie Beirach and also studied briefly with Sofia Rosoff.

Roberta has performed professionally as a sidewoman with David Liebman, Rufus Reid, Michael Formanek, Lionel Hampton, Mickey Roker, Harvey Wainapel, Eliot Zigmund, Billy Mintz, and the BMI/New York Jazz Orchestra, and has twice been a featured guest on *Marian McPartland's Piano Jazz*, on National Public Radio.

Roberta has taught at Long Island University and has several private students at the Berkeley-Carroll School in Brooklyn. She has also held master classes and/or clinics at the Eastman School of Music, California Institute of the Arts, Rutgers University, Duke University, as well as many other institutions in the U.S., Europe, and Japan.

Roberta has six CDs as a leader which have frequently made the jazz magazines' yearly top ten lists. She currently leads two bands: The *Roberta Piket Trio* and *Alternating Current*. *Piano & Keyboard* recently called Roberta "one of the most accomplished and inventive young jazz pianists currently working on the scene."

More information about Roberta's music can be found at her web sites: www.RobertaJazz.com and www.AlternatingCurrent.info.

Foreword

Many instrumentalists wish to pursue jazz improvisation, but are intimidated because they don't know what notes to play over chord changes, beyond the chord tones themselves. Frequently students who do know what scales they need to learn in order to play over changes are unable to internalize this information to the point of being able to use the scales in an actual playing situation. They may have difficulty learning the notes because they are unsure of what fingerings to use, or they may not have had enough guidance in making the transition from *playing* the scales to *applying* them in a musical situation.

If you are working on blues progressions, or just want to be more comfortable soloing on dominant seventh and dominant seventh sus chords, this book should be very useful for you. It provides fingerings and notes for the Mixolydian mode in all twelve keys. More importantly, it offers a workbook approach to applying the Mixolydian mode to jazz improvisation with melodic examples that you can practice. You can listen to these examples on the Muse Eek website as well. You will also learn how to incorporate approach notes into your playing, how to practice the blues, and how and when to use sus chords. The goal is to provide you with enough guidance to work confidently on your own so that you become comfortable integrating the use of the scales into your improvisation.

This book is part of a series (available as e-books or in paper format) that will focus on learning and applying jazz scales in order to give you the vocabulary and skill to become a fluid jazz improvisor.

Muse Eek Publishing has created a website with a FAQ forum for this book. If you get stuck, or have questions or feedback, please contact me at Roberta@muse-eek.com and I will be happy to respond in the forum.

Roberta Piket
Brooklyn, New York

How To Use This Book

The material in this section has already been presented in previous volumes of the *Jazz Piano Vocabulary* series. If you have studied any of those books you may wish to skip this section. You may find it useful to review, however, in order to brush up on your practice habits.

This series of books assumes that you know how to read music and that you have a basic understanding of the diatonic (major/minor) system. If you need to brush up on your note-reading or diatonic scales, there is an extensive primer in *Jazz Piano Vocabulary: Volume 1 - The Major Scale* on note-reading, intervals, triads, seventh chords and rhythmic notation. If you find anything in this book confusing, please visit the Muse Eek web site at www.muse-eek.com first and check the FAQ section for this book to see if your question has already been answered. If not, use the form on the website to e-mail your questions.

A note on terminology: Occasionally the word *scale* will be used in this book interchangeably with the word *mode*. I usually employ the word *scale* only when discussing general concepts. When discussing a specific mode (such as the G Mixolydian mode, for example) I will use the word *mode*.

The purpose of this book is to help you improve your ability to improvise using the Mixolydian mode. Since you are learning a new skill, reading the book and understanding the material intellectually are not enough. It is critical that you memorize the scales and fingerings and practice the examples repeatedly until you have mastered them. Execute each example at the piano slowly and carefully to begin. Increase your tempo gradually as your ability increases.

You may wish to use a metronome to be certain that you are not slowing down on difficult passages. Try putting the metronome on the "two and four"; that is, the second and fourth beats of each measure. This emphasis on the "weak" beats instead of the "strong" first and third beats is part of what gives jazz its unique rhythmic character. If it is too difficult for you to play with the metronome on two and four, then first learn the scales with the metronome on the quarter note and then, after you are comfortable with the notes, try the "two and four" again. Eventually it will get easier to feel the music this way and your sense of rhythm will become stronger and more sophisticated.

Play through each exercise smoothly and evenly. As you master each exercise you should gradually increase the tempo while still maintaining complete control. This will help you to develop good habits which will remain with you when you start playing more technically challenging music.

This book contains a great deal of material. You will not be able to learn everything in the book in one sitting. Depending on how fluent you are with scales in general, it may take you anywhere from a few weeks to several months or more to truly master the exercises in this book. Spend as much time as you need on each exercise until you have truly mastered it.

Consistency is critical. Even if you have less time on some days than on other days, it is extremely important that you refresh your memory almost every day until the material is completely absorbed. If you do this, you will find that you will progress much more steadily and will save yourself a great deal of frustration.

In the same vein, it is also a good idea to go back to previous material even while moving forward through the book. This will help reinforce what you've already learned, enabling you to build on it. For example, if you have learned the first six Mixolydian scales and are working on the seventh, you may want to play through the first six at least once a day until they become second nature so that you don't forget them.

Swung Eighth Notes

Each scale is presented in an eighth note pattern (resolving to a quarter note at the top and bottom) to allow for an even four-bar phrase as the scale ascends and descends. If you are comfortable doing so, try to play each exercise with *swung eighth notes* so that this type of feel can become second nature to you. In swung (or "swinging") eighth notes, the first eighth note in a pair of eight notes is held twice as long as the second eighth note, giving the notes a relaxed triplet feel. Eighth notes are almost always interpreted in jazz music as *swung*. For example, note the following phrase:

In a jazz context, this would be played as:

Example 1

Obviously, it would be very cumbersome to write every single eighth note pair in a lead sheet as a triplet. For this reason, in jazz it is assumed that the eighth-note is swung unless otherwise noted. Two exceptions to this rule are Brazilian jazz and Latin jazz where it is understood that the eighth notes are *straight* (that is, not swung).

A sound file illustrating this example has been provided on the Muse Eek website under this book's title.

Order of Presentation

The scales are ordered by key using the *circle of fifths*. The circle of fifths allows us to progress through all the keys by moving either up or down in perfect fifths from one key to the next. The fifth is the only interval by which we can move up or down through all the keys without repeating any key. If you do not understand intervals such as a fifth, please see the "Reading and Theory Basics" section in Volume 1 of this series.

In the scales section of this book we will progress down in fifths, from C Mixolydian to F Mixolydian to Bb Mixolydian, etc., until we arrive at the last scale, G Mixolydian.

Fingering

Often inexperienced pianists find it difficult to know which finger to use on which key. The fingerings that are provided in this book are intended to keep you from "running out of fingers" as you play ascending and descending lines.

Fortunately, fingering notation for piano is standardized throughout all genres of music. The thumb of each hand is always "1", and the pinky is always "5". If you can remember this then you will quickly become proficient at applying the correct fingerings as you learn to play a passage of written music.

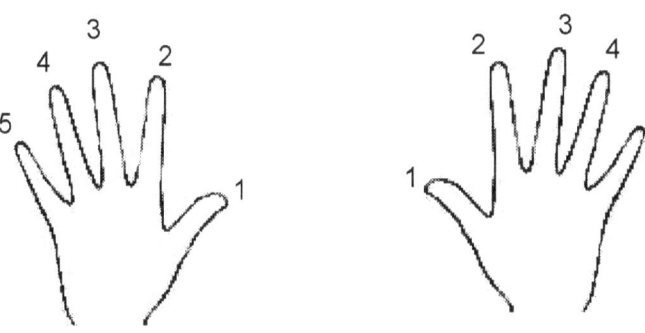

Particularly if you are self-taught, some of these fingerings may at first seem awkward. Give yourself a chance to get used to them. After learning them, if something still feels awkward, you can change it. Everyone's hand is different. However, don't assume they don't work if they feel "funny" the first time you try them. Practice them slowly, making sure to apply them accurately and consistently. Only by applying the correct fingerings every time you play will using them become automatic. Eventually, with enough experience, you will be able to determine the correct fingering on your own.

Introduction To The Mixolydian Mode

The modes that developed in Europe during the Medieval period are surprisingly useful in jazz improvisation. These modes are sometimes known as the "Church modes" because they evolved through the use of Gregorian chant, the sacred monophonic music of Europe's Catholic Church during this period. The Church modes are derived from the Major scale. That is, each mode has the same notes as the Major scale, but each mode starts and ends on a different note from the Major scale. The seven modes that we use in jazz are: Ionian, Dorian, Phrygian, Lydian, Mixolydian, Aeolian, and Locrian.

This book is concerned with the Mixolydian mode. Below we will see how the notes of the Mixolydian mode fit over both dominant seventh chords and dominant seventh suspended chords, making this mode useful for improvising on these chords.

The Mixolydian mode can be derived by starting and ending on the fifth note of a major scale. For example, the G Mixolydian mode starts on G and contains all the notes in the C major scale from G to G:

Because the G Mixolydian mode uses the notes of the C Major scale, C Major is referred to as the *parent scale of G Mixolydian.* By knowing the parent scale of a mode, it is easy to figure out the notes that belong to that mode. As another example, if we want to figure out how to play an E Mixolydian mode, we would first want to understand that E is the fifth degree of the A Major scale, making A Major the parent scale of E Mixolydian. Note that all the notes below are found in A major:

Understanding the relationship of the Mixolydian mode to its parent scale will help you understand the mode's use and will make it easier to learn the notes of each mode. However, this is merely an intermediate step. The goal is to hear and relate to the G Mixolydian mode *as* a G Mixolydian mode, *not* as a C major scale starting on G. If you do not learn to think and hear beyond C Major when you play G Mixolydian, you are adding an extra step which will interfere with your ability to hear and react instantaneously to whatever chord you encounter when improvising. (If you have trouble hearing the modes and chords and how they relate to each other you may find it helpful to investigate one or more of the ear-training books on the Muse Eek website.)

Another way to think of the Mixolydian mode is in terms of its sequence of whole steps and half steps. (A half step is the distance between two notes that are right next to each other on the piano, such as A and B flat, or B and C. A whole step is simply two half steps. Major and minor scales, and the modes derived from these scales, always consist of combinations of these two intervals. (For a more detailed explanation of these fundamental music theory concepts please examine the theory primer at the beginning of Volume 1 of this series.)) The pattern of steps for any Mixolydian mode in any key is the same:

whole step whole step half step   whole step whole step half step whole step

You may notice that this pattern is the same as that of a Major scale with the seventh degree lowered by a half step. For many musicians keeping this in mind is the easiest way to derive the Mixolydian modes, at least until you know them by memory.

Applying The Mixolydian Mode To Improvisation

There are two types of seventh chords to which we will apply the Mixolydian mode. One is the dominant seventh chord. The second is the dominant 7th sus 4 chord (or just "dominant 7th sus"). Both of these chords are discussed below.

Dominant Seventh Chord Tones

If we ascend the Mixolydian mode in thirds, we derive the first, third, fifth and seventh notes of the scale:

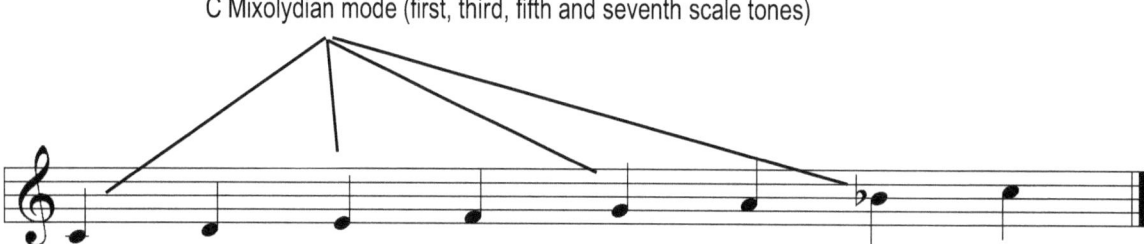

When played together these notes make up a C dominant seventh chord:

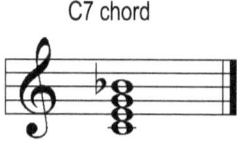

Dominant Seventh Chord Tensions

If we continue up the Mixolydian mode in thirds, we arrive at the upper extensions of a dominant seventh chord. Upper extensions (also called *tensions*) are notes above the chord tones that can be added to the chord in order to make the chord sound more interesting:

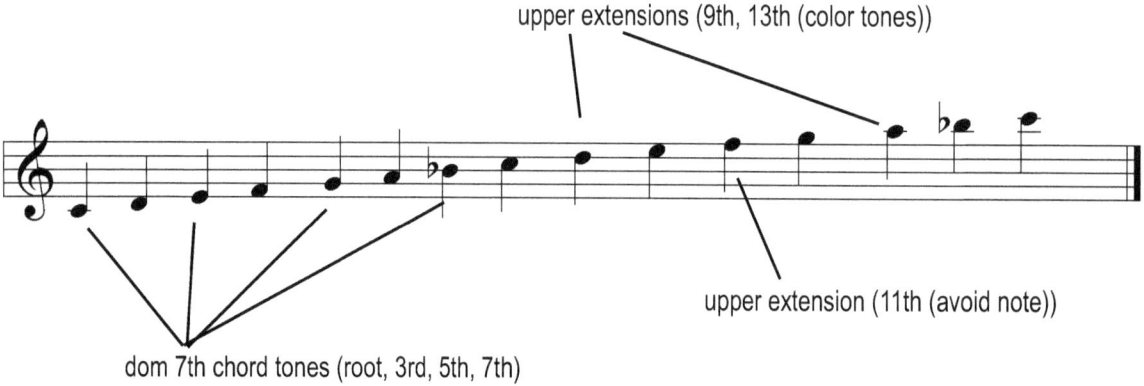

The first upper extension is the ninth. If we continue up in thirds we arrive next at the 11th and then at the 13th. The 9th and 13th are also known as color tones because they add tonal shading to the chord. They do not change the characteristic sound of the chord, which is primarily determined by the root, third and seventh of the chord. For this reason, it is common for pianists to add a 9th and/or 13th to a dominant seventh chord even if the chord symbol in the music does not specify them. The 9th and 13th can be used freely when improvising over a dominant 7th chord.

The 11th is not considered a possible color tone for a dominant seventh chord because it changes the characteristic sound of the chord. If it is placed right next to the third of the chord, the 11th can impart a harmonic muddiness that is not characteristic of a dominant seventh chord. For this reason, the 11th is considered an *avoid note* when improvising over a dominant seventh chord. An avoid note does not mean that the note can never be used. It does indicate that the note should resolve to a chord tone or a color tone rather than being held without this resolution.

Above we have examined the relationship of the notes in the Mixolydian mode to the dominant 7th chord. As you can see from this examination, a Mixolydian mode can be used to improvise over its corresponding dominant seventh chord. The example above uses the C Misolydian mode, but these relationships are, of course, the same for any key. For example, a D Mixolydian Mode can be used to play over a D dominant seventh chord, an A Mixolydian mode can be used over an A dominant seventh chord, etc.

Suspended Chord Tones

You may already be familiar with sus chords, but in case you are not, we will briefly go over them before we see how they relate to the Mixolydian scale.

"Sus" or "Sus 4" is an abbreviation for a *suspended four* chord. This refers to a major triad in which the third (the middle note) is raised a half step or "suspended", "waiting" to resolve back down to the third.

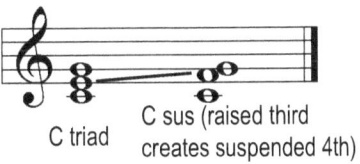
C triad   C sus (raised third creates suspended 4th)

If we add a minor third on top of a sus 4 triad we create a *dominant seventh sus* chord.

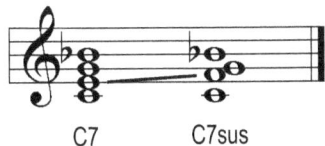
C7   C7sus

This chord is frequently used as a substitution chord for a dominant seventh chord in post-modern jazz. As we will soon see, it can also be used as a substitute for a ii chord in the standard jazz ii-V7 chord progression.

All of the material below applies to both dominant 7th sus chords and to sus 4 triads.

Just as we derived the dominant seventh chord tones from the Mixolydian scale in the previous section, we can derive the notes of the dominant seventh sus chord:

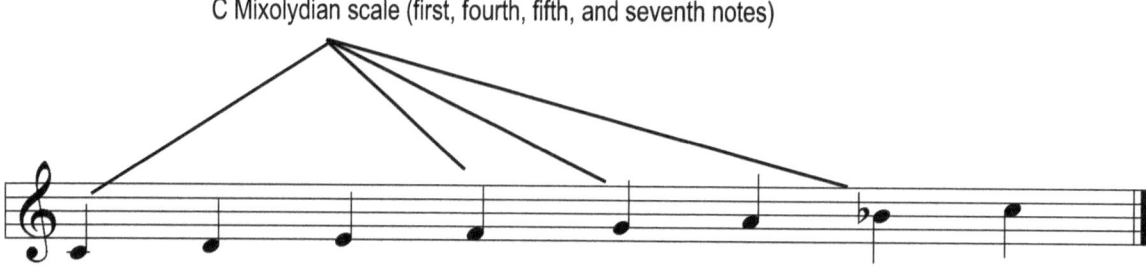

Let's look at the upper extensions of a dominant seventh sus chord that can be derived using the Mixolydian mode:

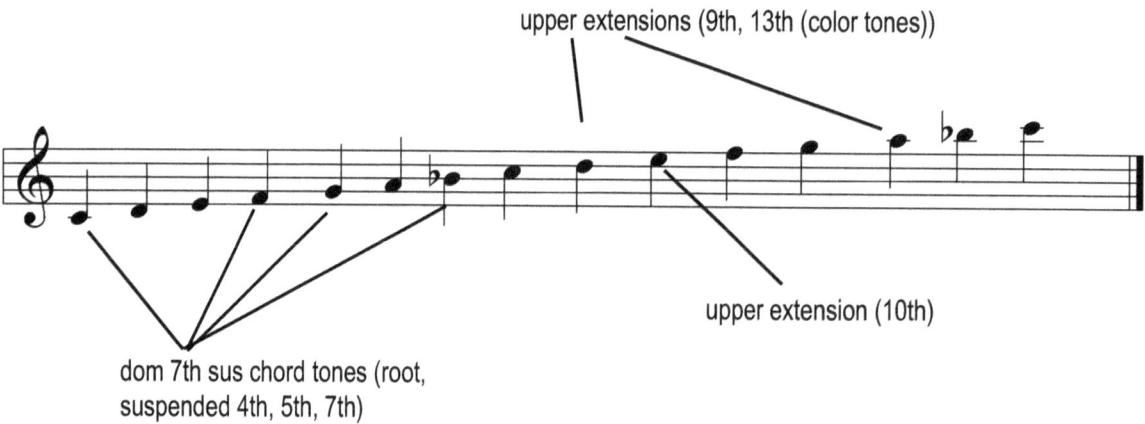

Suspended Chord Tensions

Because of the suspension in the chord, there is no third. However, when the third is displaced by an octave, it creates a major tenth. Like the 9th and 13th, the tenth works as an upper extension in chord voicings and soloing for the dominant seventh sus chord.

You will notice that the 11th is the same note as the fourth. Because the fourth is a chord tone in the dominant seventh sus chord, the 11th is <u>not</u> considered an avoid note on this chord, and should be used like all the other chord tones in the dominant seventh sus chord. Thus, there are no avoid notes in the Mixolydian scale when soloing over a dominant seventh sus chord.

Explanation Of Left Hand Chord Voicings

Once you are comfortable playing the modes in your right hand, the next step is to learn the corresponding seventh chord in the left hand. Eventually you will play these left-hand voicings while playing the mode in the right hand. There are many other possible voicings you can play over these chords. The ones provided are standard voicings that will be extremely useful to learn.

Two left-hand chord voicings are provided for you to accompany yourself while playing the corresponding mode in the right hand. One is a voicing for the dominant seventh chord and the other is a voicing for the dominant seventh sus chord.

Dominant Seventh Voicings

The dominant seventh chord voicing we will use employs the 3rd, 13th, 7th and 9th of the dominant seventh chord. For example, a D7 voicing could be played as follows in the left hand:

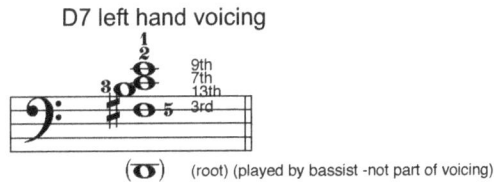

The root in this chord is not meant to be played on the piano. It is only provided so that you can hear the chord against its root. This type of "rootless" voicing is useful to learn because, when you are playing with a bass player in a real-world situation, it is not always necessary to play each chord's root. The bass player will do that for you (usually).

Why do we use the 13th in this voicing when we could just as easily have moved this note (the B in the D7 chord) down a whole step to give us the fifth instead? Generally speaking, the fifth of the chord is not critical to identifying the quality of the chord. By substituting the color tone of the natural 13th, we get a more interesting left hand voicing. As we learned earlier, it is generally considered permissible and often desirable for the pianist to add tensions such as the ninth and thirteenth to a dominant seventh chord, even if they are not specified in the chord symbol. When no tensions are specified in the chord symbol, the decision regarding which tensions to add is based on whether or not the tension will clash with the melody that is being played above the chord. Thus, the pianist must use his or her ears (listening to the soloist) and/or eyes (reading the melody on the page) to determine which tensions are appropriate.

There are other tensions that are available on the dominant seventh chord. For example, depending on the melody being played over the chord, a flat 13th or a flat 9th might be appropriate. In the example below, we have flatted the 13th:

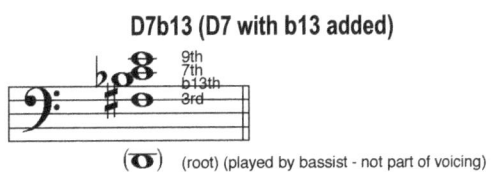

These tensions, while very useful and important to eventually know, are not available in the Mixolydian scale. For this reason, we will not treat them in detail in this book. There are other scales which can be used when dealing with dominant seventh chords which do contain b9 and/or b13 chord tensions. These include the *Lydian b7, altered, half-whole diminished* (also known as *symetrical diminished*), *whole tone, Mixolydian b2, b6* as well as more obscure scales such as the *double-augmented*. They will be addressed in other volumes. For now we will use the natural 9th and natural 13th as our only tensions, because these are the tensions that exist in the Mixolydian mode. Thus, if you are using the Mixolydian mode to improvise, playing a left hand voicing with natural 9th and natural 13th will not clash with the notes you are using in your right hand.

For some of the left hand voicings, the order of the notes has been changed (inverted) so that the left hand will not sound too high or too low on the keyboard. For example, in a G dominant seventh chord, voicing the chord tones in order (from the 3rd up) will get in the way of the right hand. However, if we invert the chord so that the top two notes (the 7th and 9th) are placed *under* the 3rd and 13th then there will be more room for the right hand:

G7 left hand voicing

Dominant Seventh Sus Voicings

A rootless dominant seventh sus voicing is provided to the right of the dominant seventh voicing for each scale, using the fourth, thirteenth, seventh and ninth of the chord. If you have previously explored Volume 2 of this series, you may recognize this as containing the same intervallic pattern as the voicings we used in that book for the minor seventh chord. By moving the bass note down a perfect fifth, the name of the chord is changed. For example, what was our G-7 chord becomes a C dominant seventh sus chord if we move the root down a fifth.

As you can see, it is very useful to learn these left hand voicings because they can be utilized in many different harmonic contexts.

The Dominant Seventh Sus Chord As a Passing Chord

This section will be easier for you to understand if you have a basic understanding of functional harmony. If it is confusing to you, you can safely skip it without effecting your ability to work through the rest of the material in the book.

Earlier we mentioned that a sus chord is often used in post-modern jazz as a substitution for the dominant 7th chord (depending on the melody and the style of the piece). The sus chord can also be used as a passing chord leading to the dominant seventh chord. (A passing chord is a chord which we can insert before a functional chord in order to create more harmonic movement and interest.) Because the eleventh in the dominant seventh sus chord is a suspension of the third, it creates a very satisfying resolution to go from the dominant seventh sus to the dominant seventh:

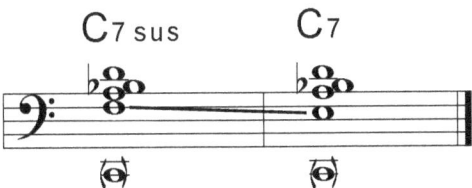

Let's take this two-chord progression and add one more chord to it. As you may be aware, V-I is the most common progression in music. Most people can hear the resolution of a V chord to a I chord even if they cannot name it. (For more information on diatonic chords in the major keys and their Roman numerals, please see the theory primer in Volume 1 of this series.) Since C dominant 7th is the V chord in the key of F major, we can resolve the C7 chord to the I chord which is F major 7th:

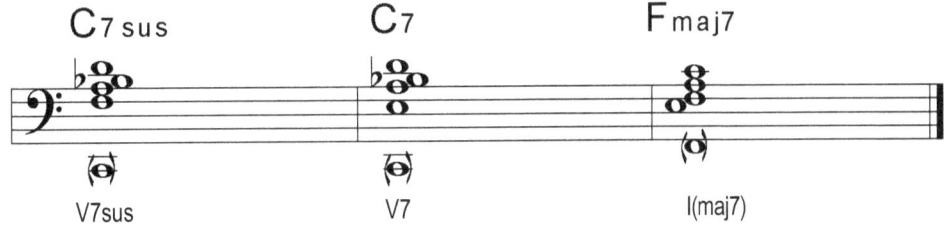

Above, we saw that a sus7 chord uses the same voicing as the minor seventh chord a perfect fifth above it. For this reason, we can view our passing C7sus chord as G-7/C (G-7 over a C bass note). G-7 is the ii chord in the key of F major. Therefore, by putting the G-7/C before the C7 chord, we are essentially creating a ii-V7-I progression. Below is the same progression again, with the exception that the root of the first chord is G instead of C.

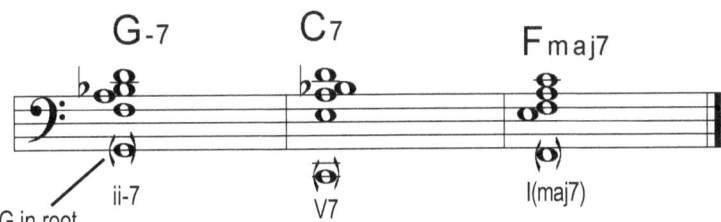

Because the only difference between the two progressions is this bass note, we can see that, in a ii-V7 or ii-V7-I progression, we can use the dominant 7th sus chord built on the fifth degree of the key (V7sus) as a substitute for the ii-7 chord.

When you are working on chord progressions for various tunes, you can practice inserting the dominant 7th sus chord as a passing chord or as a substitute ii-7 chord when you see dominant 7th chords or ii-V7 progressions. The etude presented later in this book uses dominant 7th sus chord in these ways.

Mixolydian Modes: Fingerings And Left Hand Chord Voicings

Before you get started working on the scales, here are a few suggestions and guidelines to help you get the most out of your practice time.

Hand Position

It is important to develop good habits with respect to hand position. It may not seem important when playing slowly, but when you begin to execute faster passages, you will find that good hand and wrist position will make a difference in your control, thus effecting your ability to play evenly and cleanly.

When playing notes that are close together, as is the case with scales, fingers should be bent, so that you are playing with the balls of your fingers. (If you have long finger nails you will need to cut them to achieve this.) All fingers should be kept in this rounded position whether you are using them or not. (See the picture below.) Of course if you are playing a widely spread chord, your fingers will not be as bent as they are when playing a scale in which each note is adjacent to the next note to be played. The idea is to keep your fingers in a gently bent yet relaxed position.

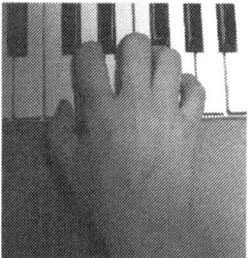

Many inexperienced pianists veer their wrists from side to side, particularly when changing hand position as they go up and down the keyboard while playing a scale. In medical circles this is known as ulnar deviation and is a great way to develop wrist tendonitis (a bad thing). When changing hand position as you ascend or descend the keyboard, do NOT change your wrist position relative to your hand. Instead, as your arm glides up (or down) the keyboard, bring your thumb under you hand and reach for the note. Let your thumb do the stretching, not your wrist. Keep your elbows close to your side

Practice Method

To begin, practice each scale in the right hand, up two octaves and down two octaves, paying attention to the fingering provided. (Right hand fingering is notated above each note of the scale.) You may find it useful to say each note out loud as you play. Even better for your ear is to try to sing the notes of each scale while playing.

The reason why you should initially focus on learning each scale in your right hand is that once you learn the notes you will be accompanying yourself with the appropriate chord in your left hand, much as your left hand would "comp" while your right hand solos. As a matter of good training and technique, however, it is valuable to master all the Mixolydian modes with both hands. For this purpose, left hand fingerings for each Mixolydian mode are provided (below each note).

Dynamics

Keep in mind that the left hand is *accompanying* the right hand. Therefore, the left hand should be a bit softer than the right hand. At first it may seem difficult to coordinate your hands in this way, but if you try to *hear* the right hand melody louder, as opposed to merely trying to play harder with your right hand, then eventually you will naturally begin to emphasize the melody more.

Using The Left Hand Chord Voicings

Once you are comfortable playing the scales in your right hand, the next step is to play the corresponding seventh chord voicing in the left hand while playing the scale in the right hand. As discussed in the previous section, it is suggested that you practice all twelve of the Mixolydian modes against the dominant seventh chord; then practice all the Mixolydian modes again against the dominant seventh sus chord.

After you learn the scale you will be ready to add the chord voicing in the left hand. The bass note in parentheses below the chord indicates the root of the chord. While you would not play this note in an actual playing situation, it is useful to hear the root when practicing. Play the root with your left hand and sustain it with the damper (sustain) pedal, then lift your hand and play the first rootless voicing (the dominant seventh chord) as written. While holding this chord with your left hand, take your foot off the damper (sustain) pedal and play the scale in your right hand. This technique will help you hear the chord from the bottom up, allowing you to get its tonality in your ear. It will also enable you to aurally relate the scale to the chord. (Note: This is for practice only. Do not play and hold the root in an actual playing situation.)

When playing each chord, identify each chord tone in your mind as 3rd, 7th, 9th or 13th.

After you have gone through this process for all twelve of the dominant seventh voicings, repeat the same steps with the second voicing for all twelve of the dominant seventh sus chords. The dominant seventh sus chord is positioned in the second measure for legibility only. You should play this chord the same way that you played the dominant seventh chords, holding down the chord and then playing the entire scale in your right hand up and down two octaves. Again, make sure you can identify each chord tone, this time as 4th, 7th, 9th or 13th.

Swung Eighth Notes, Articulation and Phrasing

Playing these scales with a swung eighth note feel (as explained in the "How To Use This Book" section) will help you to develop a more authentically "jazz" rhythmic feel.

As you become more comfortable with the actual notes of each scale and chord, you should begin to focus more on the subtleties of articulation. Each scale should be played legato, meaning that the notes are connected. Many jazz piano students make the mistake of trying to play too staccato (disconnected and short), because of the percussive nature of jazz. However, do *not* use the damper or sustain pedal when playing medium tempo or faster jazz eighth note lines. This is another common error made by inexperienced pianists.

The Modes

C Mixolydian mode

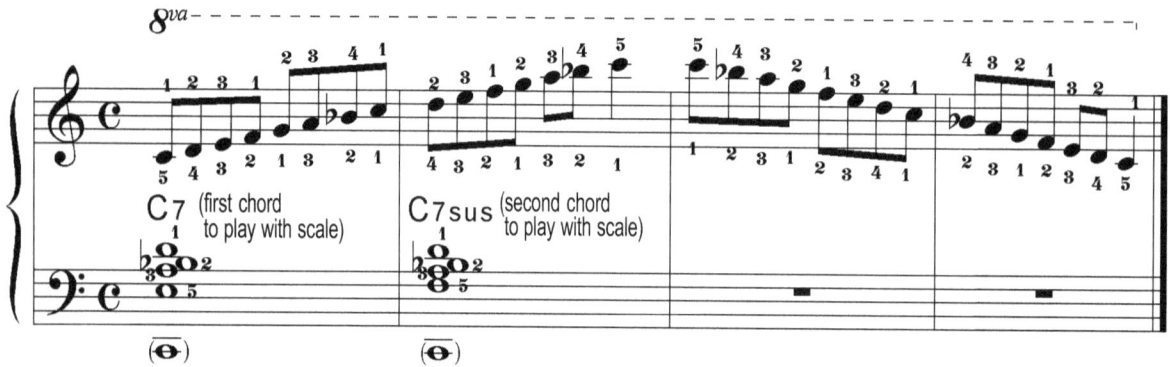

F Mixolydian mode

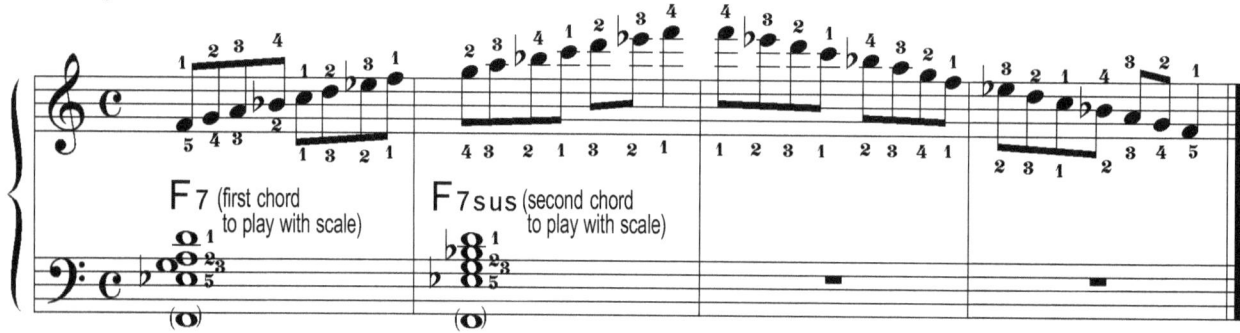

Bb Mixolydian mode

Eb Mixolydian mode

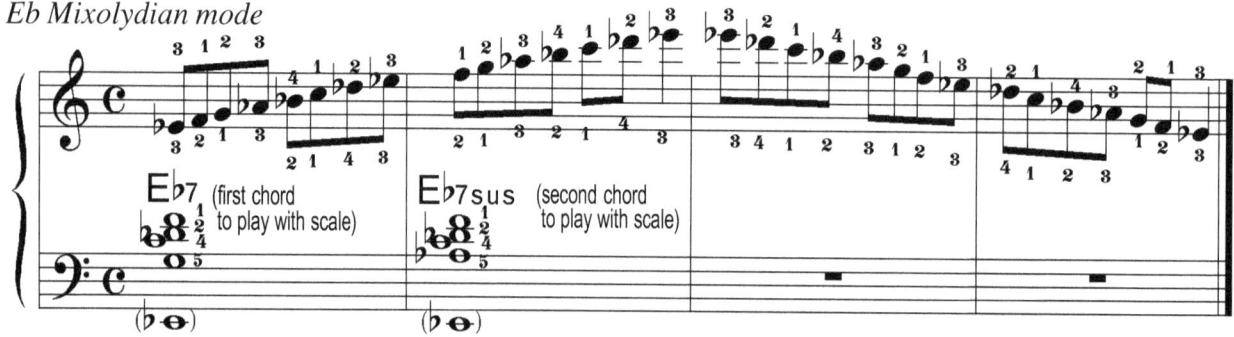

Ab Mixolydian mode

Db Mixolydian mode

F# Mixolydian mode

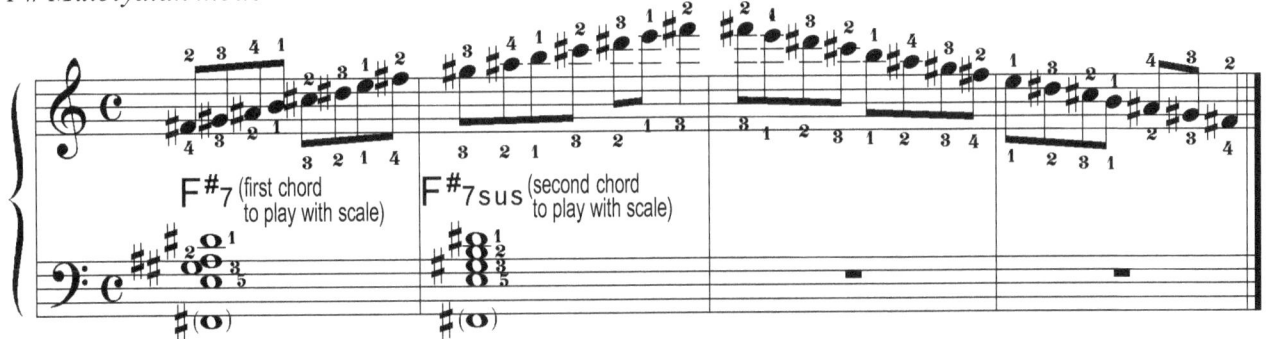

B Mixolydian mode

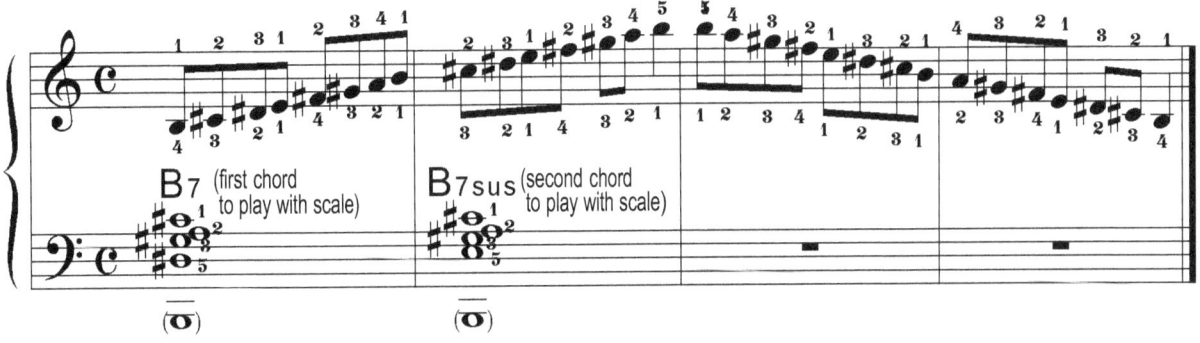

E Mixolydian mode

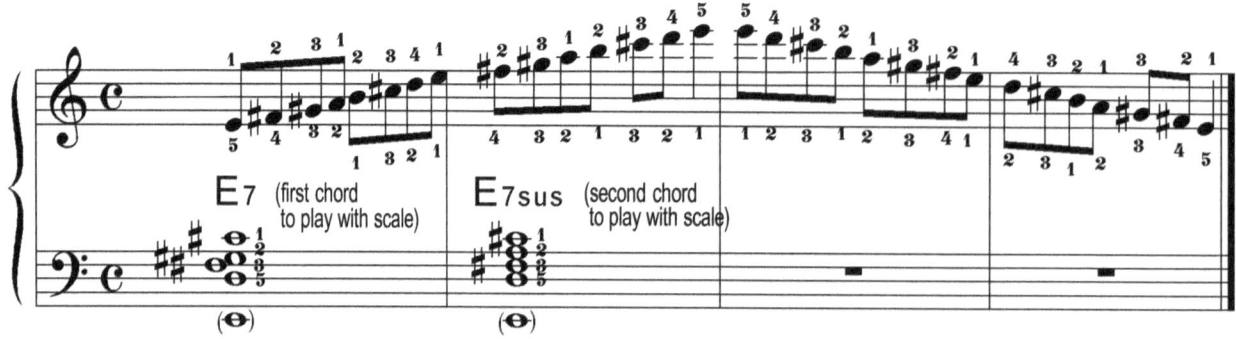

A Mixolydian mode

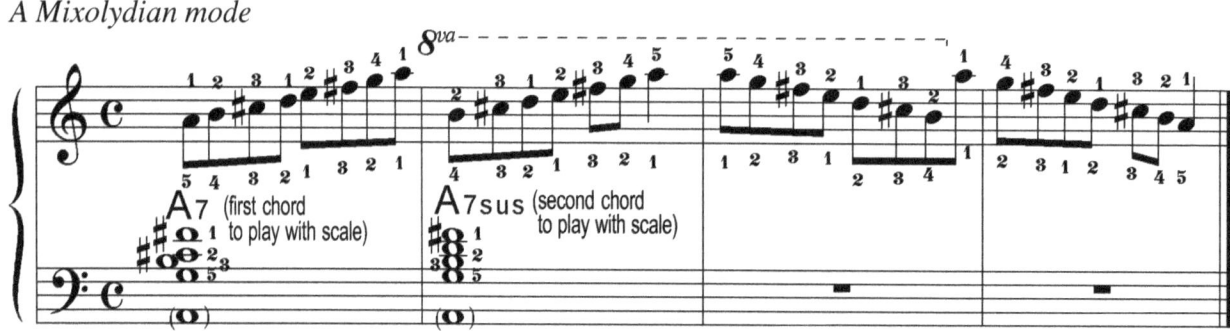

D Mixolydian mode

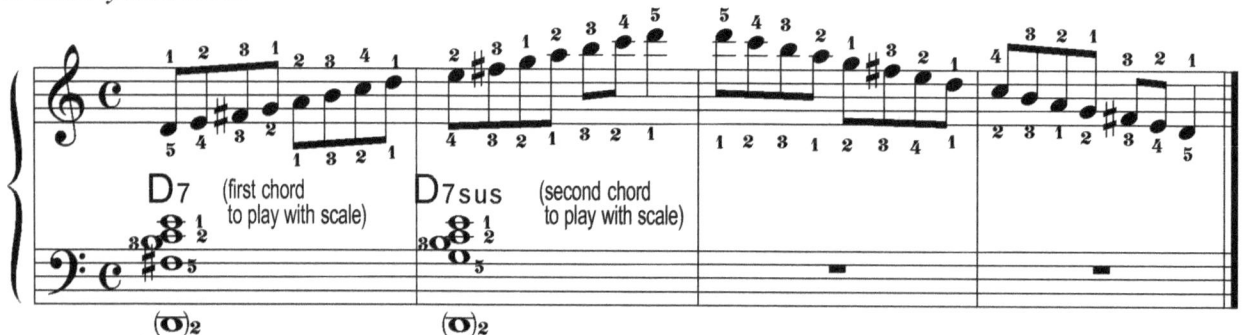

G Mixolydian mode

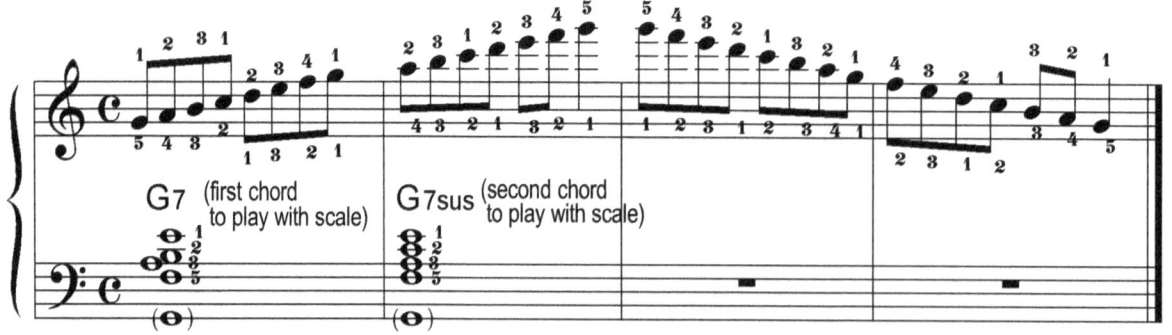

Examples of Melodic Lines Using the Mixolydian Mode

After you have mastered the Mixolydian mode in all keys, you will want to try improvising using this new material. A multitude of examples of melodic lines derived from the Mixolydian mode have been provided to get you started thinking melodically. Try to play each line in several different keys. This will help you better understand the relationship between the notes and the chord and will improve your assimilation of the material.

You will notice that the melodic lines in this section consist almost entirely of eighth notes. This is because the ability to play steady, swinging eighth-note lines is so important to playing jazz. While it is tempting to add lots of sixteenth notes as your chops develop, they will not sound good if you cannot lay down a simple melodic idea with a solid rhythmic feel underneath it. As Duke Ellington famously put it, "it don't mean a thing if it ain't got that swing."

Sound files of the examples below are located on the Muse Eek website under this book's title. Listening to these audio files and playing along with them will help you develop a better sense of the steady swinging eighth-note feel you should be trying to develop in your playing.

As we discussed earlier, the eleventh is considered an *avoid note* when improvising over a dominant seventh chord. An avoid note does *not* mean the note can never be used. It *does* indicate that the note should resolve to a chord tone or a color tone rather than being held without this resolution. The following melodic lines will work over both a dominant 7th chord or a dominant 7th sus chord because they do not contain a non-resolving 11th.

All fingerings are for the right hand.

Dominant Seventh Chord Ideas

Example 5

Example 6

Example 7

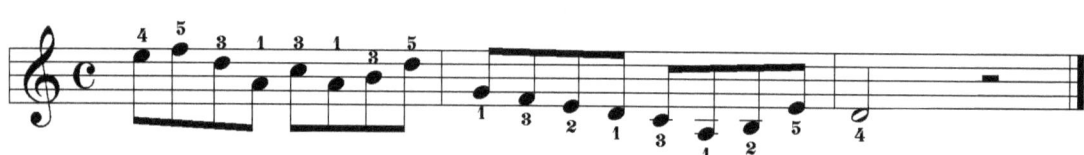

Example 8

Example 9

Dominant 7th Sus Chord Ideas

Because the following melodic sequences use the 11th without resolving it to a chord tone or tension, they would not sound characteristic of a dominant seventh chord. However, they work fine over a dominant 7th sus chord because the 11th is the same as the 4th in the sus 4 chord.

If you wish to hear this for yourself, try changing the chord quality in the examples below to a dominant 7th chord instead of the indicated dominant 7th sus chord. While the dissonance that is created may appeal to you, it is not characteristic of the sound of a dominant 7th chord and should only be used with that caveat in mind.

Example 10

Example 11

Example 12

Your Ideas

On the following pages, space is reserved for you to create your own melodic lines using the Mixolydian mode. Writing out your ideas slows down the process, allowing you time to better understand what you are doing. Another advantage of writing down your lines is that over time you will have a written record of your improved understanding of these concepts.

The goal of all this is, of course, to be able to improvise comfortably using this new vocabulary. Towards this end it is important to do *some* improvising every day. Even if you can only play a G Mixolydian scale to begin with, you should try improvising over it. At first it may not sound good to you, but it will only get better if you practice it.

When you write out and play your own practice lines on the blank staves below, be aware of which lines contain avoid notes that make them better suited to use over a sus chord than a dominant seventh chord. Think about which tensions you are using and what they sound like in relation to the chord's root.

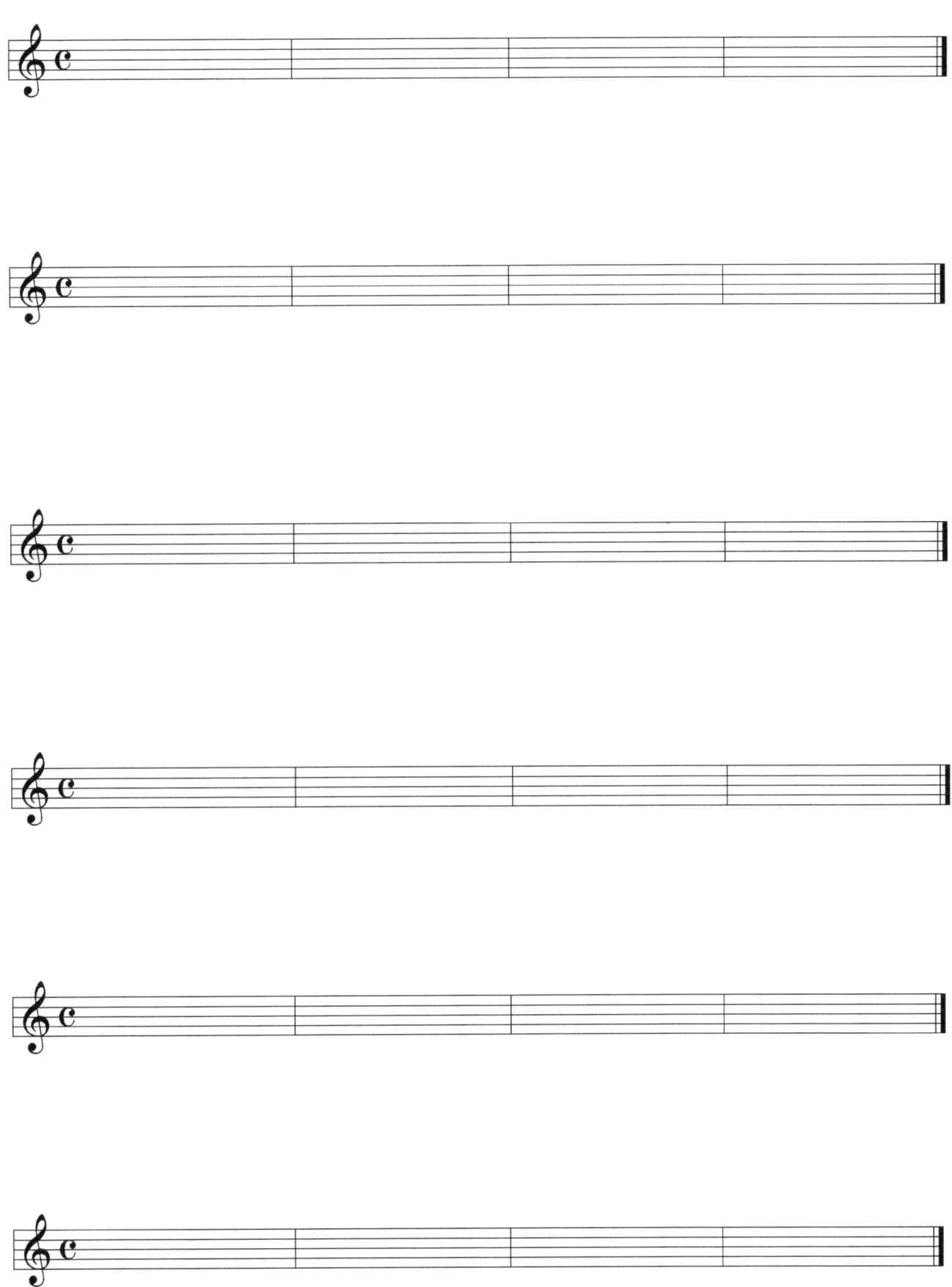

An Introduction To Approach Notes

Approach notes are notes that are next to a target note and resolve to that note. The target note can be a chord tone or a chord tension. In this book we will illustrate the use of approach notes resolving to chord tones that fall on the beat, since this is the way approach notes are used in Be-bop jazz. In later volumes we will discuss more advanced uses of approach notes to lead into chord tensions.

There are two types of approach notes. *Diatonic approach notes* are notes in the chord's scale that are next to and resolve to a target chord tone or tension. The circled notes in the example below are diatonic approach notes. They are approach notes because they each resolve to a target note next to them. They are diatonic because they are all contained within a scale of the chord (in this case, C Mixolydian):

Example 13

The second type of approach note, the *chromatic approach note*, seen below in Example 14, is a note that is always a half step away from a target note, and leads into it. Because they are always a half step away from the scale tone, chromatic approach notes frequently occur outside of the chord's scale. Therefore, chromatic approach notes may be diatonic in some instances but not in others. In the example below, the circled notes are chromatic approach notes:

Example 14

In Be-bop, approach notes are frequently used to lead into chord tones which can appear on any of the four quarter note beats of the measure. Here are some more examples of lines which use both chromatic and diatonic approach notes in this way. Play through these lines to get a sense of what they sound like and how they look and feel on the keyboard.

Example 15

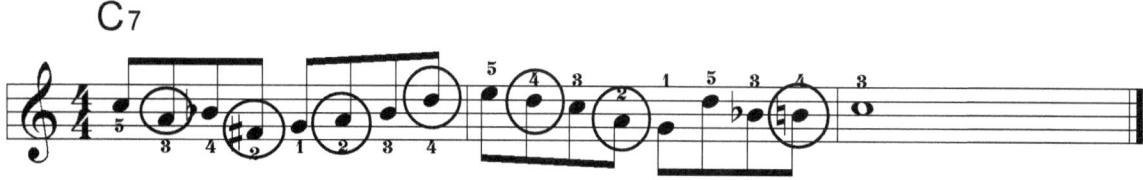

28

Example 16

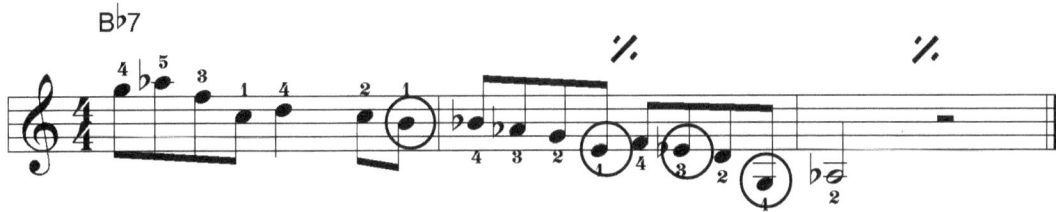

A double approach occurs when a note leads into another note which then resolves in the same direction to the target note. In the following example, Eb approaches D, which then resolves to Db, a chord tone of the Eb7 chord:

Example 17

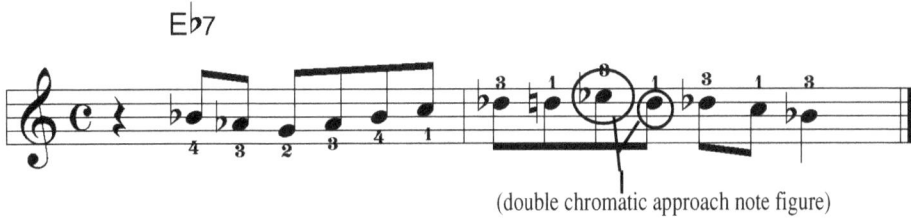

(double chromatic approach note figure)

When playing Be-bop lines, it is best to avoid *starting* an approach note figure from a non-diatonic note when resolving downward. For this reason the example below would not sound appropriate in a Be-Bop setting:

Example 18

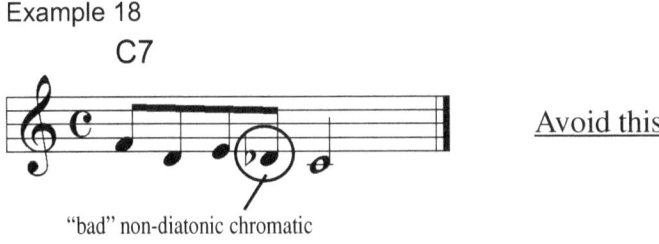

"bad" non-diatonic chromatic approach from above - avoid for now

Avoid this.

The following example works because even though F is an approach note resolving downward to the chord tone E, F is also diatonic to the Mixolydian scale:

Example 19

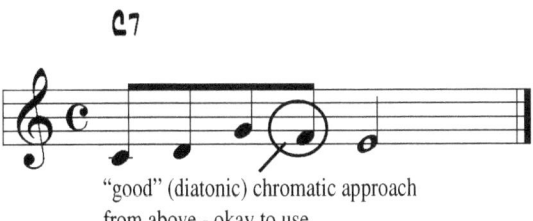

"good" (diatonic) chromatic approach from above - okay to use

Above we have stated a general rule: While an approach note from below the target note can start on a non-diatonic note, an approach note from above should start only on a diatonic note. This general guideline will get you started using approach notes that sound "right" in a Be-bop context. Keep in mind, however, that over time you will become experienced enough to understand how to "break" the rules and still sound convincing. A proficient improvisor can make less common approach notes work in every style of jazz. Below we will discuss some exceptions to the "descending approach note" rule. Until you feel confident using these exceptions, stick to the simple rule of avoiding downward-resolving non-diatonic approach notes.

It is acceptable to use a descending non-diatonic approach note when the following exception occurs: If the descending non-diatonic approach note is not the starting note, but is preceded by an acceptable approach note pattern leading into it, it will sound good. In the following example, the F# and G lead into the Ab approach, making the Ab leading to the G sound acceptable in a Be-bop context:

Example 20

Another example of an acceptable non-diatonic approach note pattern resolving downward is this double approach in which the non-diatonic chromatic approach (Ab) is preceded by a diatonic approach note (A):

Example 21

Here is one last example of an acceptable approach note pattern using chromatic non-diatonic approach notes resolving downward. In this example the target note (E) is preceded by a pattern consisting of an approach from one direction (F), and then from the other direction (D#).

Example 22

There are scales other than the Mixolydian mode which can be played over a dominant seventh chord. If you are using one of these scales, some chromatic approach notes which are not diatonic to the Mixolydian mode will be diatonic to these scales. However, until you are ready to learn these other scales, it is best to be aware of whether a descending chromatic approach note is diatonic to the Mixolydian mode before considering how to use it, or whether to use it at all.

Play all of the examples above on your keyboard. Transpose them into several keys. This will help you to get the sound of approach notes in your ear.

In order to get comfortable incorporating approach notes into your playing, apply them to any chord you are practicing playing over. Below is a discussion of how to practice using approach notes.

Let's get started with a C7 chord. First we will review C7 arpeggiated (broken) inversions ascending and descending the keyboard without concerning ourselves with approach notes:

Example 23

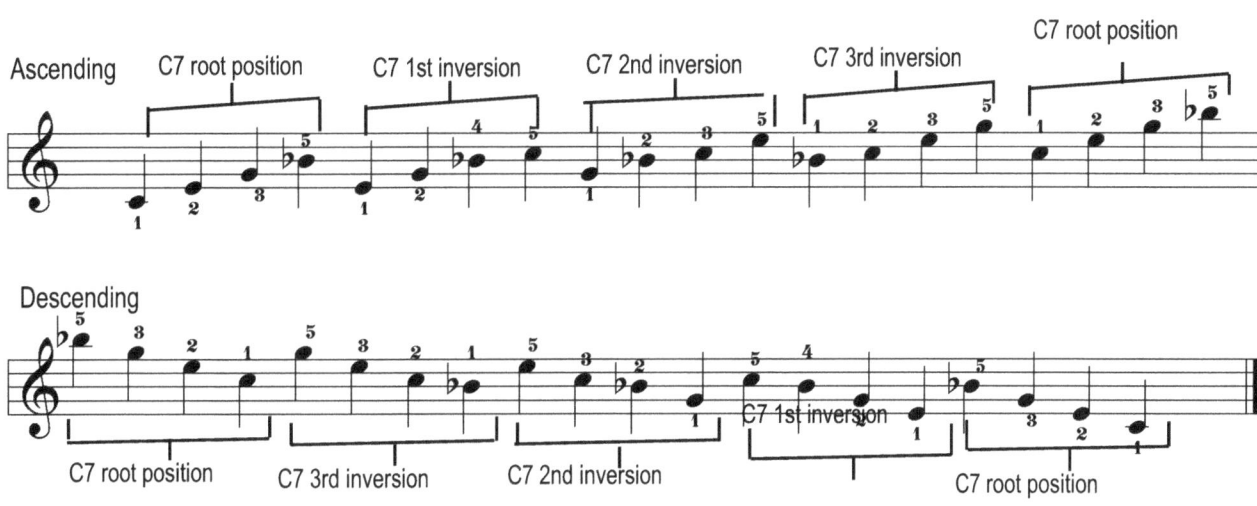

Now we will play C7 arpeggios with an approach note inserted. We will begin by inserting an approach note below C. Since B is a half step below C, the chromatic approach below C is B. Here is the same C7 arpeggio series as above with B inserted as an approach note to each C:

Example 24

As another example, below is an arpeggiated C7 chord with a chromatic approach note leading to the 3rd of the chord:

31

Example 25

Ascending

Descending

Above we inserted a chromatic approach note before the 3rd of the chord. Now let's insert the *diatonic* approach note below the 3rd of the chord. In the Mixolydian scale, D is the diatonic approach note below E. Here is the same arpeggated series with the diatonic approach note leading up to the 3rd of the C7 chord:

Example 26

Ascending

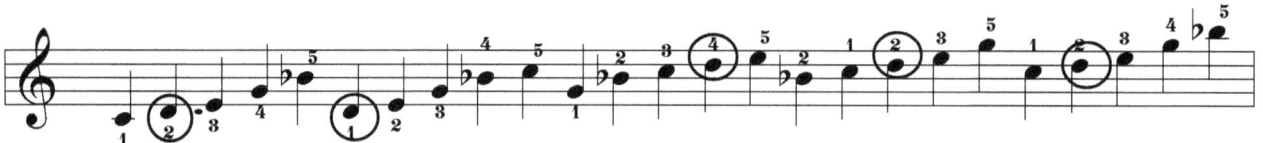

Descending

Space is provided on the following pages for you to write out your own ideas and exercises using approach notes. You may also find it useful to write in fingerings. Those that you especially like you should transpose into several keys. If you do these exercises as part of your daily practice consistently and with great awareness over a period of weeks or months, you will begin incorporating approach notes into your playing without thinking about it consciously while you are playing.

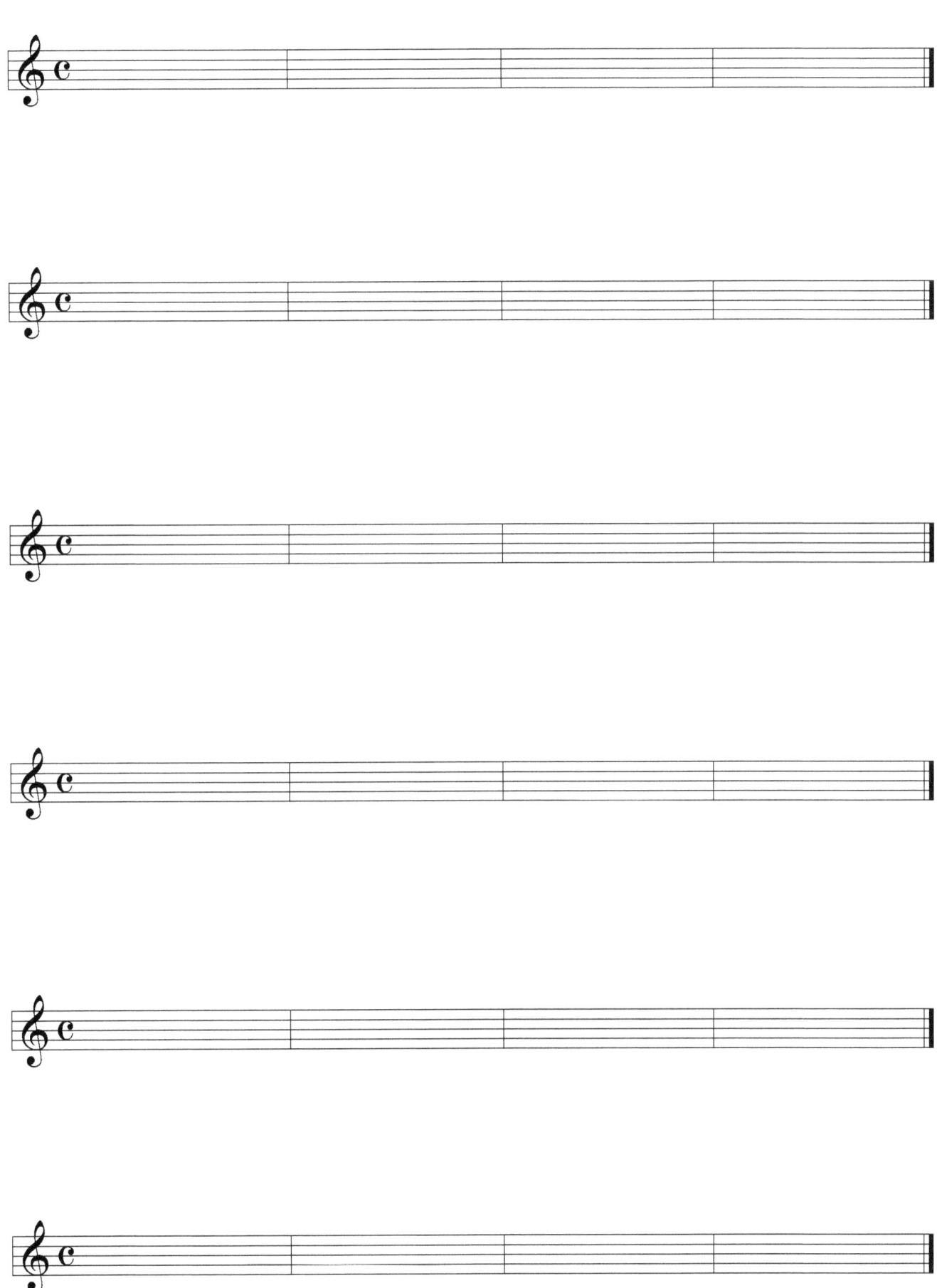

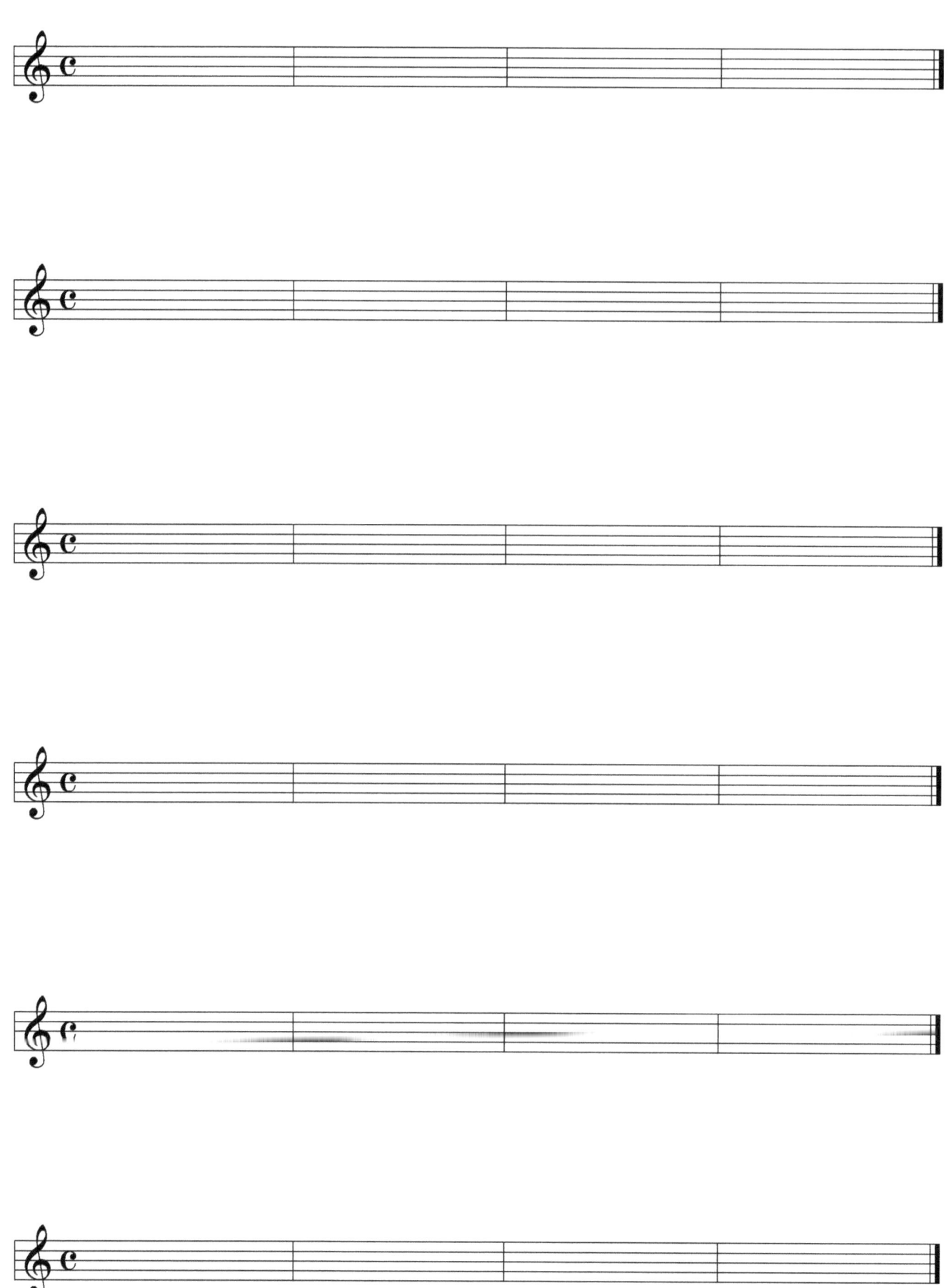

The Blues

The Blues is a style of music which originated in the field hollars and shouts of African-American slaves and developed as an expression of the experience of African-Americans primarily in the American south through the early 20th century. The twelve-bar blues is a musical form (or template) which is common in the Blues genre. In the Jazz genre, twelve-bar blues is a commonly used form which illustrates jazz's roots in the Blues.

The Blues Scale

The scale that developed out of the early blues is known as the *Blues Scale*. In relation to the major scale, it consists of the tonic (the first note of the scale), the flatted 3rd, the 4th, the flatted 5th, the natural 5th, and the flatted seventh.

C Blues Scale - Two Octaves

The most important aspect of the twelve-bar blues progression is that, in keeping with the melodic alterations in the Blues scale, all of the chords in the harmonic progression are traditionally of the dominant seventh chord quality. For example, normally in a major key we would expect the I ("one") chord to be a major seventh chord; however, in a blues progression it is typically a dominant seventh. Therefore, in a C blues, the I chord would be C7.

The same is true for the quality of the IV ("four") chord. In a blues progression the quality of the IV chord is dominant seventh instead of the major seventh quality that we would expect to see on the IV chord in a major key. On a blues progression in the key of C major, this gives us an F7 chord which contains Eb. As we saw above, while Eb is not found in the C major scale, it is found in the C Blues scale.

Because of its use of dominant seventh chords, the twelve-bar blues progression is a useful way to practice soloing using the Mixolydian scales. While you can also use the Blues scale to solo over the blues progression, you should be aware of the Mixolydian scale when playing over a blues. The Mixolydian scale will give your soloing a more mainstream jazz sound and broader harmonic palette, as opposed to the more old-fashioned "bluesy" sound of the Blues scale.

Basic Blues Form

The standard twelve-bar blues form consists of three musical phrases, each of four measures. Below, this form is illustrated in the key of C major. In the most basic version of the blues form, the first bar consists of the I chord, followed by the IV chord in the second bar. The third and fourth bar return to the I chord. (In the case of a C blues, the I chord is of course C7). The chords in the fifth and sixth bar of the blues are IV chords of the dominant seventh quality (in this case, F7). There is a return to the tonic (the I) chord in the seventh and eighth bars.

The last line of the basic blues form consists of a bar on the V chord, followed by a bar on the IV chord, returning to I on the last two chords. Thus, a traditional 12 bar blues in C Major would look like this:

Example 27

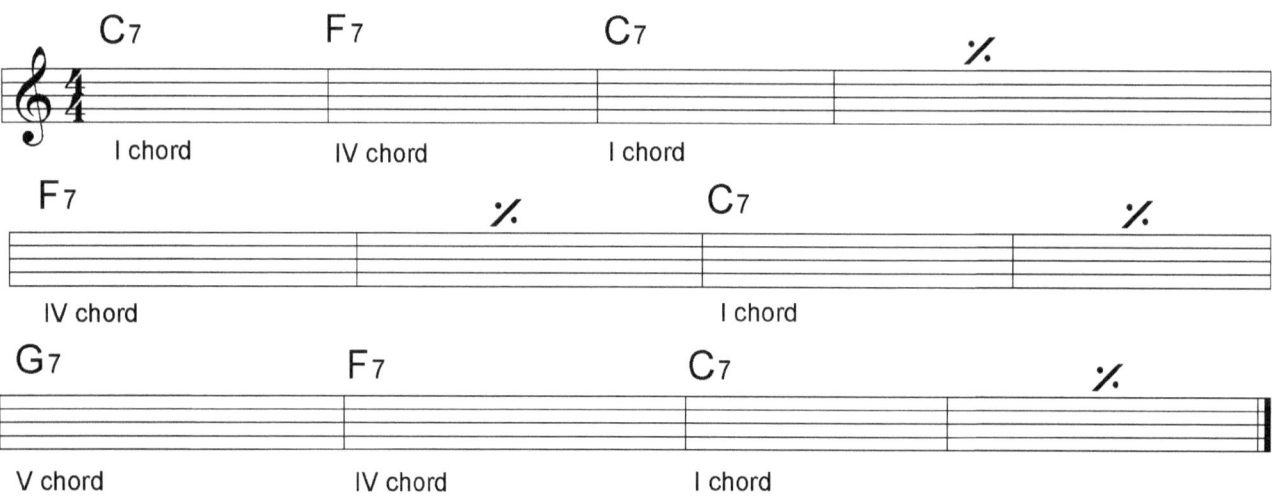

The 12-bar blues form is a very common form and as a jazz improvisor you would do well to memorize this form and learn to solo over it in all keys. C, F, and Bb are especially common keys in which you will see blues pieces written. For this reason these are good keys to start with.

There are many standard substitutions and variations on the basic blues form which you will eventually encounter and learn. This basic form is just a starting point, but it is the foundation for all the variations you will encounter in the future.

Keeping The Form

If you have trouble following the form while playing, try practicing by repeating four bars at a time over and over. When you feel comfortable with four bars, try to play over eight bars at a time without losing your place. If you work on this consistently you will find that it gets easier to keep your place in the form while also following the chord changes. Eventually you will develop an internal sense of form so that you will know what bar you are on without counting. A MIDI file of these chords will be found on the Muse-Eek website under this book's title if you wish to play along.

Listening To The Blues

There are many pieces in jazz written on variations of the basic blues chord progression. For exploration of blues progressions as used in modern jazz, you may wish to explore tunes such as

Blue Monk (Thelonious Monk), *Some Other Blues*, *Bessie's Blues* (both by John Coltrane), *Billie's Bounce, Blues For Alice* (both by Charlie Parker), *Blues On The Corner* (McCoy Tyner), Isotope (Joe Henderson) as well as countless others. There are also many minor blues such as *Mr. P.C.*, *Equinox* (both by Coltrane), and *Israel* (Bill Evans).

You may also wish to go to the source and listen to some Blues artists from the early part of the 20th century such as singers Ma Rainey, Big Joe Turner, and Bessie Smith, guitarist/singers Blind Lemon Jefferson, Leadbelly and Robert Johnson, guitarist John Lee Hooker, cornetist W.C. Handy, stride pianists Jelly Roll Morton, Willie 'The Lion' Smith and James P. Johnson, and boogie woogie pianists Meade Lux Lewis and Albert Ammons.

Mixin' It Up: A Mixolydian Etude On The Blues

In the piece on the following page (Example 28) there are a few modifications to the basic blues form we have learned. First, we have added a four-bar introduction which is not part of the blues form. This introduction is labeled on the chart.

The next modification we have made is to insert dominant 7th sus chords as passing chords before the dominant seventh chords. Then, in bar 13, instead of a straight-forward G7 chord, we use G7b13. We use the flatted 13th because the natural 13 would conflict with the Eb in the melody. (To simplify the solo form, the G7b13 in bar 13 has been replaced in the blowing changes with a G7 chord.) In bar 14, instead of F7, we use F dominant 7th sus. Again, the chord was changed to fit the melody which contains a non-resolving Bb (an avoid note on the F dominant 7th chord!). On the last bar (bar 16) we have changed the I chord to a V chord (G7b13). This is because the piece repeats back to the beginning of the twelve bar blues form. The V chord at the end leads us back to the I chord at the beginning of the form.

When you first start working on this piece, you may find it helpful to focus on the right hand, and leave out the left hand voicings and rhythms. A MIDI file containing the left hand part (both head and solo sections) has been provided so that you can play along with it. After you learn the melody and feel comfortable soloing, you can try adding the left hand. If this is too challenging, you may find it easier to simply play half notes in the left hand, instead of the syncopated rhythm indicated. For example, bar 18 looks like this:

But you could also play it like this, making it easier to improvise over:

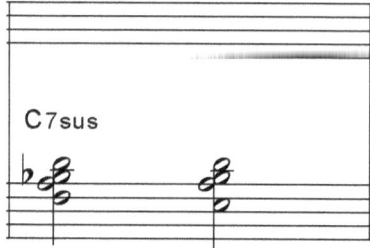

Learn this piece and other blues tunes you encounter in several keys. Practice will help you master the blues form and will allow you to work on soloing over many different dominant 7th and dominant 7th sus chords. This piece is Example 28. In addition to a MIDI file, an audio file is available on the Muse-Eek website under this book's title page.

Mixin' It Up

R. Piket

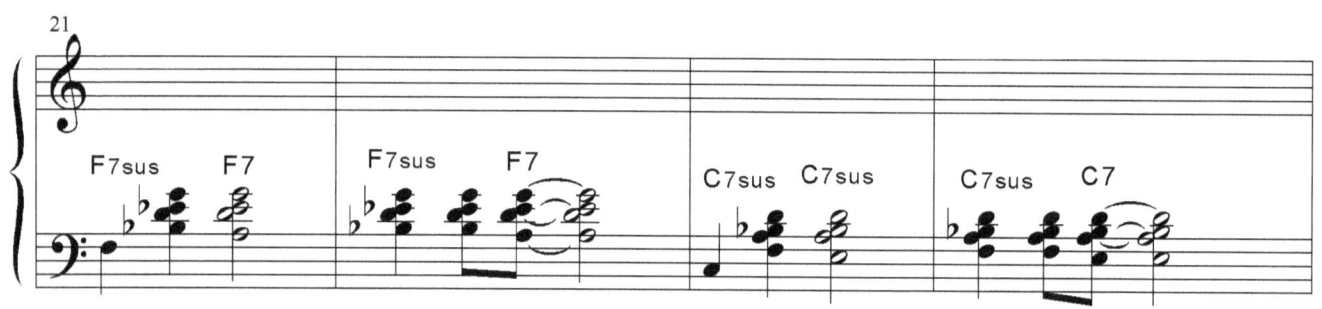

Further Exploration

To get a better sense of how you want to sound as you explore jazz improvisation, it is important to listen to jazz. I have found that many inexperienced players do not have a sense of where to find the right music to listen to.

In Volume 2 of this series, I included an extensive jazz piano disography. In the current volume, I have supplemented this list with some additional jazz piano and keyboard recordings which you may find helpful and inspiring to listen to. There are several artists on this list who were not included on the previous list. I have also added CDs from masters who were included, as well as some CDs with electric keyboard playing such as Wurlitzer and Fender Rhodes pianos and Hammond B3 Organ. Once again I issue the disclaimer that this supplemental list is not intended to be comprehensive, as that would require an entire book in itself. Rather, it is a selection of various styles from early jazz to contemporary jazz. It also reflects my own biases and preferences. If one of these artists grabs your ear, then seek out other recordings by that artist.

Many of the musicians on these recordings are still performing. If you have the chance to hear them live, especially in a smaller venue, there is no substitute for the knowledge you will gain by closely observing the ideas, technique, touch, and stage presentation of a master.

Please remember that those artists who are still alive have poured their respective hearts and souls into recording their music. They may rely on record sales to help support their artistry. If you copy CDs instead of purchasing them you are hindering their ability to create their music for you in the future.

Supplemental Cross-Sectional Jazz Piano Discography

Early Jazz, Swing and Blues
Fats Waller: The Definitive Fats Waller - Volume 1 (Jazz Classics)
Meade Lux Lewis: The Blues Piano Artistry of Meade Lux Lewis (Original Jazz Classics)
Albert Ammons: Boogie Woogie Man (Asv Living Era)
James P. Johnson: Harlem Stride Piano 1921-1929 (Epm Musique)

Big Band and Swing
Duke Ellington: Piano Reflections (Capital Jazz)
Duke Ellington: Ellington At Newport 1956 (Columbia)
Duke Ellington and Count Basie: First Time: The Count Meets The Duke (Columbia)
Earl Hines: Piano Man! (Asv Living Era)

Be-Bop
Thelonious Monk: Monk's Dream (Sony)
Thelonious Monk: Solo Monk (Columbia)
Bud Powell: The Scene Changes (Blue Note)

Bud Powell: Bouncing With Bud (Delmark)
Walter Bishop, Jr.: Speak Low (Muse)

Post-Bop to Post-Modern
Art Blakey and the Jazz Messengers (with Horace Silver): A Night At Birdland (Blue Note)
Larry Young: Unity (Blue Notes)
Dexter Gordon (with Sonny Clark): Go! (Blue Note)
Red Garland: Red Garland's Piano (Original Jazz Classics)
Wynton Kelly: Kelly Blue (Riverside)
Wynton Kelly and Wes Montgomery: Full House (Riverside)
Dorothy Donegan: The Explosive Dorothy Donegan (Audiophile)
Miles Davis (w/ Red Garland): Relaxin' (Original Jazz Classics)
Sonny Rollins (w/ Tommy Flanagan): Saxophone Colossus (Original Jazz Classics)
Cannonball Adderly (w/ Hank Jones): Somethin' Else (Blue Note)
Dave Brubeck: Time Out (Columbia)
Bill Evans: A Simple Matter Of Conviction
Bill Evans: Alone (Verve)
Bill Evans: Intuition (Original Jazz Classics)
Joe Henderson (with McCoy Tyner): Inner Urge (Blue Note)
Joe Henderson (with Cedar Walton): Mode For Joe (Blue Note)
Joe Henderson (with Kenny Barron): The Kicker (Milesstone)
Herbie Hancock: Mwandishi: The Complete Warner Bros. Recordings (Warner Bros.)
Paul Bley: Fragments (ECM)
George Cables: Cables' Vision (Original Jazz Classics)
Fred Hersch: Plays Monk (Nonesuch)
Joanne Brackeen: Fi-Fi Goes To Heaven
John Hicks: Naima's Love Song (Diw Records)
Richie Beirach: Trust (Evidence)
Kenny Barron: Live At Bradley's (Sunnyside)
Eliane Elias: The Three Americas (Blue Note)
Stanley Cowell: Brilliant Circles (Black Lion)
Renee Rosnes: As We Are Now (Blue Note)
Steve Kuhn: Mostly Ballads (New World Records)

Fusion/Electric Jazz
Miles Davis (w/ Chick Corea, Joe Zawinul, Larry Young): Bitches Brew (Sony)
Chick Corea: Light As A Feather (Polygram)
Chick Corea: The Leprechaun (Polygram)
Tony Williams (w/ Larry Young): Emergency! (Polygram)
Joe Zawinul: Zawinul (Atlantic)
John McLaughlin and Mahavishnu Orchestra (w/ Jan Hammer): Inner Mounting Flame (Columbia)
Herbie Hancock: Headhunters (Columbia)
Herbie Handcock: Thrust (Sony)
John Abercrombie (with Jan Hammer): Timeless (ECM Records)

What Next?

If you have worked through this book you should be comfortable using the Mixolydian scale to improvise over dominant seventh chords and dominant seventh sus chords. You will be on your way to developing a strong sense of blues form and feeling comfortable playing over this form in several keys. You will also have begun improvising more sophsticated lines through the use of approach notes.

It is important to remember that truly mastering the material may be a process that takes place over a long period of time. Work on the material in this book or, even better, develop and practice your own ideas based on this material, on a regular basis until the information and the skills you have gained become second nature. You may wish to look at some of the online material in the members area of the Muse Eek website which includes some left hand comping rhythms, theory, sound samples of the examples, and other helpful information.

This book is part of a series of books that focuses on learning and applying jazz scales in order to give you the vocabulary and confidence to become a fluid jazz improvisor. When you are ready, you may wish to build on the progress you've made by choosing another book in this series.

There are so many directions to explore in music, it can seem overwhelming. Your practice time should not seem like a chore which you must drag yourself through for a certain amount of time each day. Rather, music is a perpetual adventure with discoveries always waiting. I hope that you will remain inspired for the rest of your life.

Books Available From
Muse Eek Publishing Company

The Bruce Arnold series of instruction books for guitar are the result of 20 years of teaching. Mr. Arnold, who teaches at New York University and Princeton University has listened to the questions and problems of his students, and written forty books addressing the needs of the beginning to advanced student. Written in a direct, friendly and practical manner, each book is structured in such as way as to enable a student to understand, retain and apply musical information. In short, these books teach.

1st Steps for a Beginning Guitarist
Spiral Bound ISBN 1890944-90-4   Perfect Bound ISBN 1890944-93-9

"1st Steps for a Beginning Guitarist" is a comprehensive method for guitar students who have no prior musical training. Whether you are playing acoustic, electric or twelve-string guitar, this book will give you the information you need, and trouble shoot the various pitfalls that can hinder the self-taught musician. Includes pictures, videos and audio in the form of midifiles and mp3's.

Chord Workbook for Guitar Volume 1 (2nd edition)
Spiral Bound ISBN 0-9648632-1-9   Perfect Bound ISBN 1890944-50-5

A consistent seller, this book addresses the needs of the beginning through intermediate student. The beginning student will learn chords on the guitar, and a section is also included to help learn the basics of music theory. Progressions are provided to help the student apply these chords to common sequences. The more advanced student will find the reharmonization section to be an invaluable resource of harmonic choices. Information is given through musical notation as well as tablature.

Chord Workbook for Guitar Volume 2 (2nd edition)
Spiral Bound ISBN 0-9648632-3-5   Perfect Bound ISBN 1890944-51-3

This book is the Rosetta Stone of pop/jazz chords, and is geared to the intermediate to advanced student. These are the chords that any serious student bent on a musical career must know. Unlike other books which simply give examples of isolated chords, this unique book provides a comprehensive series of progressions and chord combinations which are immediately applicable to both composition and performance.

Music Theory Workbook for Guitar Series

The world's most popular instrument, the guitar, is not taught in our public schools. In addition, it is one of the hardest on which to learn the basics of music. As a result, it is frequently difficult for the serious guitarist to get a firm foundation in theory.

Theory Workbook for Guitar Volume 1
Spiral Bound ISBN 0-9648632-4-3   Perfect Bound ISBN 1890944-52-1

This book provides real hands-on application of intervals and chords. A theory section written in concise and easy to understand language prepares the student for all exercises. Worksheets are given that quiz a student about intervals and chord construction using staff notation and guitar tablature. Answers are supplied in the back of the book enabling a student to work without a teacher.

Theory Workbook for Guitar Volume 2
Spiral Bound ISBN 0-9648632-5-1   Perfect Bound ISBN 1890944-53-X

This book provides real hands-on application for 22 different scale types. A theory section written in concise and easy to understand language prepares the student for all exercises. Worksheets are given that quiz a student about scale construction using staff notation and guitar tablature. Answers are supplied in the back of the book enabling a student to work without a teacher. Audio files are also available on the muse-eek.com website to facilitate practice and improvisation with all the scales presented.

Rhythm Book Series

These books are a breakthrough in music instruction, using the internet as a teaching tool! Audio files of all the exercises are easily downloaded from the internet.

Rhythm Primer
Spiral Bound ISBN 0-890944-03-3   Perfect Bound ISBN 1890944-59-9

This 61 page book concentrates on all basic rhythms using four rhythmic levels. All examples use one pitch, allowing the student to focus completely on time and rhythm. All exercises can be downloaded from the internet to facilitate learning. See http://www.muse-eek.com for details

Rhythms Volume 1
Spiral Bound ISBN 0-9648632-7-8   Perfect Bound ISBN 1890944-55-6

This 120 page book concentrates on eighth note rhythms and is a thesaurus of rhythmic patterns. All examples use one pitch, allowing the student to focus completely on time and rhythm. All exercises can be downloaded from the internet to facilitate learning. See http://www.muse-eek.com for details.

Rhythms Volume 2
Spiral Bound ISBN 0-9648632-8-6   Perfect Bound ISBN 1890944-56-4

This volume concentrates on sixteenth note rhythms, and is a 108 page thesaurus of rhythmic patterns. All examples use one pitch, allowing the student to focus completely on time and rhythm. All exercises can be downloaded from the internet to facilitate learning. See http://www.muse-eek.com for details.

Rhythms Volume 3
Spiral Bound ISBN 0-890944-04-1   Perfect Bound ISBN 1890944-57-2

This volume concentrates on thirty second note rhythms, and is a 102 page thesaurus of rhythmic patterns. All examples use one pitch, allowing the student to focus completely on time and rhythm. All exercises can be downloaded from the internet to facilitate learning. See http://www.muse-eek.com for details.

Odd Meters Volume 1
Spiral Bound ISBN 0-9648632-9-4   Perfect Bound ISBN 1890944-58-0

This book applies both eighth and sixteenth note rhythms to odd meter combinations. All examples use one pitch, allowing the student to focus completely on time and rhythm. Exercises can be downloaded from the internet to facilitate learning. This 100 page book is an essential sight reading tool.
See http://www.muse-eek.com for details.

Contemporary Rhythms Volume 1
Spiral Bound ISBN 1-890944-27-0   Perfect Bound ISBN 1890944-84-X

This volume concentrates on eight note rhythms and is a thesaurus of rhythmic patterns. Each exercise uses one pitch which allows the student to focus completely on time and rhythm. Exercises use modern innovations common to twentieth century notation, thereby familiarizing the student with the most sophisticated systems likely to be encountered in the course of a musical career. All exercises can be downloaded from the internet to facilitate learning. See http://www.muse-eek.com for details.

Contemporary Rhythms Volume 2
Spiral Bound ISBN 1-890944-28-9   Perfect Bound ISBN 1890944-85-8

This volume concentrates on sixteenth note rhythms and is a thesaurus of rhythmic patterns. Each exercise uses one pitch which allows the student to focus completely on time and rhythm. Exercise use modern innovations common to twentieth century notation, thereby familiarizing the student with the most sophisticated systems likely to be encountered in the course of a musical career. All exercises can be downloaded from the internet to facilitate learning. See http://www.muse-eek.com for details.

Independence Volume 1
Spiral Bound ISBN 1-890944-00-9   Perfect Bound ISBN 1890944-83-1

This 51 page book is designed for pianists, stick and touchstyle guitarists, percussionists and anyone who wishes to develop the rhythmic independence of their hands. This volume concentrates on quarter, eighth and sixteenth note rhythms and is a thesaurus of rhythmic patterns. The exercises in this book gradually incorporate more and more complex rhythmic patterns making it an excellent tool for both the beginning and the advanced student.

Other Guitar Study Aids

Right Hand Technique for Guitar Volume 1
Spiral Bound ISBN 0-9648632-6-X   Perfect Bound ISBN 1890944-54-8

Here's a breakthrough in music instruction, using the internet as a teaching tool! This book gives a concise method for developing right hand technique on the guitar, one of the most overlooked and under-addressed aspects of learning the instrument. The simplest, most basic movements are used to build fatigue-free technique. Exercises can be downloaded from the internet to facilitate learning. See http://www.muse-eek.com for details.

Single String Studies Volume One
Spiral Bound ISBN 1-890944-01-7   Perfect Bound ISBN 1890944-62-9

This book is an excellent learning tool for both the beginner who has no experience reading music on the guitar, and the advanced student looking to improve their ledger line reading and general knowledge of each string of the guitar. Each exercise concentrates the students attention on one string at a time. This allows a familiarity to form between the written pitch and where it can be found on the guitar along with improving one's "feel" for jumping linearly across the fretboard. Exercises can be downloaded from the internet to facilitate learning. See http://www.muse-eek.com for details.

Single String Studies Volume Two
Spiral Bound ISBN 1-890944-05-X   Perfect Bound ISBN 1890944-64-5

This book is a continuation of Volume One, but using non-diatonic notes. Volume Two helps the intermediate and advanced student improve their ledger line reading and general knowledge of each string of the guitar. Each exercise concentrates the students attention on one string at a time. This allows a familiarity to form between the written pitch and where it can be found on the guitar along with improving one's "feel" for jumping linearly across the fretboard. Exercises can be downloaded from the internet to facilitate learning. See http://www.muse-eek.com for details.

Single String Studies Volume One (Bass Clef)
Spiral Bound ISBN 1-890944-02-5   Perfect Bound ISBN 1890944-63-7

This book is an excellent learning tool for both the beginner who has no experience reading music on the bass guitar, and the advanced student looking to improve their ledger line reading and general knowledge of each string of the bass. Each exercise concentrates a students attention of one string at a time. This allows a familiarity to form between the written pitch and where it can be found on the bass along with improving one's "feel" for jumping linearly across the fretboard. Exercises can be downloaded from the internet to facilitate learning. See http://www.muse-eek.com for details.

Single String Studies Volume Two (Bass Clef)
Spiral Bound ISBN 1-890944-06-8   Perfect Bound ISBN 1890944-65-3

This book is a continuation of Volume One, but using non-diatonic notes. Volume Two helps the intermediate and advanced student improve their ledger line reading and general knowledge of each string of the bass. Each exercise concentrates the students attention on one string at a time. This allows a familiarity to form between the written pitch and where it can be found on the bass along with improving one's "feel" for jumping linearly across the fretboard. Exercises can be downloaded from the internet to facilitate learning. See http://www.muse-eek.com for details.

Guitar Clinic
Spiral Bound ISBN 1-890944-45-9   Perfect Bound ISBN 1890944-86-6

Guitar Clinic" contains techniques and exercises Mr. Arnold uses in the clinics and workshops he teaches around the U.S.. Much of the material in this book is culled from Mr. Arnold's educational series, over thirty books in all. The student wishing to expand on his or her studies will find suggestions within the text as to which of Mr. Arnold's books will best serve their specific needs. Topics covered include: how to read music, sight reading, reading rhythms, music theory, chord and scale construction, modal sequencing, approach notes, reharmonization, bass and chord comping, and hexatonic scales.

The Essentials: Chord Charts, Scales, and Lead Patterns for the Guitar
Saddle Stitched (Stapled) ISBN 1-890944-94-7

This book is truly essential to the aspiring guitarist. It includes the most commonly played chords on the guitar in all keys, plus a bonus of the most commonly used scales and lead patterns. You can quickly learn all the chords, scales and lead patterns you need to know to play your favorite songs-and solo over them, too! "The Essentials" doesn't stop there, though. It also includes chord progressions to help you learn how to chord songs in folk, country, rock, blues and other popular styles. The books contain loads of easy to understand diagrams of chords, scales and lead patterns so you will be up and running in no time!

Sight Singing and Ear Training Series

The world is full of ear training and sight reading books, so why do we need more?
This sight singing and ear training series uses a different method of teaching relative pitch sight singing and ear training. The success of this method has been remarkable. Along with a new method of ear training these books also use CDs and the internet as a teaching tool! Audio files of all the exercises are easily downloaded from the internet at www.muse-eek.com By combining interactive audio files with a new approach to ear training a student's progress is limited only by their willingness to practice!

A Fanatic's Guide to Ear Training and Sight Singing
Spiral Bound ISBN 1-890944-19-X   Perfect Bound ISBN 1890944-75-0

This book and CD present a method for developing good pitch recognition through sight singing. This method differs from the myriad of other sight singing books in that it develops the ability to identify and name all twelve pitches within a key center. Through this method a student gains the ability to identify sound based on it's relationship to a key and not the relationship of one note to another (i.e. interval training as commonly taught in many texts). All note groupings from one to six notes are presented giving the student a thesaurus of basic note combinations which develops sight singing and note recognition to a level unattainable before this Guide's existence.

Key Note Recognition
Spiral Bound ISBN 1-890944-30-3   Perfect Bound ISBN 1890944-77-7

This book and CD present a method for developing the ability to recognize the function of any note against a key. This method is a must for anyone who wishes to sound one note on an instrument or voice and instantly know what key a song is in. Through this method a student gains the ability to identify a sound based on its relationship to a key and not the relationship of one note to another (i.e. interval training as commonly taught in many texts). Key Center Recognition is a definite requirement before proceeding to two note ear training.

LINES Volume One: Sight Reading and Sight Singing Exercises
Spiral Bound ISBN 1-890944-09-2   Perfect Bound ISBN 1890944-76-9

This book can be used for many applications. It is an excellent source for easy half note melodies that a beginner can use to learn how to read music or for sight singing slightly chromatic lines. An intermediate or advanced student will find exercises for multi-voice reading. These exercises can also be used for multi-voice ear training. The book has the added benefit in that all exercises can be heard by downloading the audio files for each example. See http://www.muse-eek.com for details.

Ear Training ONE NOTE: Beginning Level
Spiral Bound ISBN 1-890944-12-2   Perfect Bound ISBN 1890944-66-1

This Book and Audio CD presents a new and exciting method for developing relative pitch ear training. It has been used with great success and is now finally available on CD. There are three levels available depending on the student's ability. This beginning level is recommended for students who have little or no music training.

Ear Training ONE NOTE: Intermediate Level
Spiral Bound ISBN 1-890944-13-0   Perfect Bound ISBN 1890944-67-X

This Audio CD and booklet presents a new and exciting method of developing relative pitch ear training. It has been used with great success and is now finally available on CD. This intermediate level is recommended for students who have had some music training but still find their skills need more development.

Ear Training ONE NOTE: Advanced Level
Spiral Bound ISBN 1-890944-14-9   Perfect Bound ISBN 1890944-68-8

This Audio CD and booklet presents a new and exciting method of developing relative pitch ear training. It has been used with great success and is now finally available on CD. There are three levels available depending on the student's ability. This advanced level is recommended for students who have worked with the intermediate level and now wish to perfect their skills.

Ear Training TWO NOTE: Beginning Level Volume One
Spiral Bound ISBN 1-890944-31-9   Perfect Bound ISBN 1890944-69-6

This Book and Audio CD continues the method of developing relative pitch ear training as set forth in the "Ear Training, One Note" series. There are six volumes in the beginning level series. Through practice, the student eventually gains the ability to recognize the key and the names of any two notes played simultaneously. Volume One concentrates on 5ths. Prerequisite: a strong grasp of the One Note method.

Ear Training TWO NOTE: Beginning Level Volume Two
Spiral Bound ISBN 1-890944-32-7   Perfect Bound ISBN 1890944-70-X

This Book and Audio CD continues the method of developing relative pitch ear training as set forth in the "Ear Training, One Note" series. There are six volumes in the beginning level series. Through practice, the student eventually gains the ability to recognize the key and the names of any two notes played simultaneously. Volume Two concentrates on 3rds. Prerequisite: a strong grasp of the One Note method.

Ear Training TWO NOTE: Beginning Level Volume Three
Spiral Bound ISBN 1-890944-33-5   Perfect Bound ISBN 1890944-71-8

This Book and Audio CD continues the method of developing relative pitch ear training as set forth in the "Ear Training, One Note" series. There are six volumes in the beginning level series. Through practice, the student eventually gains the ability to recognize the key and the names of any two notes played simultaneously. Volume Three concentrates on 6ths. Prerequisite: a strong grasp of the One Note method.

Ear Training TWO NOTE: Beginning Level Volume Four
Spiral Bound ISBN 1-890944-34-3   Perfect Bound ISBN 1890944-72-6

This Book and Audio CD continues the method of developing relative pitch ear training as set forth in the "Ear Training, One Note" series. There are six volumes in the beginning level series. Through practice, the student eventually gains the ability to recognize the key and the names of any two notes played simultaneously. Volume Four concentrates on 4ths. Prerequisite: a strong grasp of the One Note method.

Ear Training TWO NOTE: Beginning Level Volume Five
Spiral Bound ISBN 1-890944-35-1   Perfect Bound ISBN 1890944-73-4

This Book and Audio CD continues the method of developing relative pitch ear training as set forth in the "Ear Training, One Note" series. There are six volumes in the beginning level series. Through practice, the student eventually gains the ability to recognize the key and the names of any two notes played simultaneously. Volume Five concentrates on 2nds. Prerequisite: a strong grasp of the One Note method.

Ear Training TWO NOTE: Beginning Level Volume Six
Spiral Bound ISBN 1-890944-36-X   Perfect Bound ISBN 1890944-74-2

This Book and Audio CD continues the method of developing relative pitch ear training as set forth in the "Ear Training, One Note" series. There are six volumes in the beginning level series. Through practice, the student eventually gains the ability to recognize the key and the names of any two notes played simultaneously. Volume Six concentrates on 7ths. Prerequisite: a strong grasp of the One Note method.

Comping Styles Series

This series is built on the progressions found in Chord Workbook Volume One. Each book covers a specific style of music and presents exercises to help a guitarist, bassist or drummer master that style. Audio CDs are also available so a student can play along with each example and really get "into the groove."

Comping Styles for the Guitar Volume Two FUNK
Spiral Bound ISBN 1-890944-07-6   Perfect Bound ISBN 1890944-60-2

This volume teaches a student how to play guitar or piano in a funk style. 36 Progressions are presented: 12 keys of a Major and Minor Blues plus 12 keys of Rhythm Changes A different groove is presented for each exercise giving the student a wide range of funk rhythms to master. An Audio CD is also included so a student can play along with each example and really get "into the groove." The audio CD contains "trio" versions of each exercise with Guitar, Bass and Drums.

Comping Styles for the Bass Volume Two FUNK
Spiral Bound ISBN 1-890944-08-4   Perfect Bound ISBN 1890944-61-0

This volume teaches a student how to play bass in a funk style. 36 Progressions are presented: 12 keys of a Major and Minor Blues plus 12 keys of Rhythm Changes A different groove is presented for each exercise giving the student a wide range of funk rhythms to master. An Audio CD is also included so a student can play along with each example and really get "into the groove." The audio CD contains "trio" versions of each exercise with Guitar, Bass and Drums.

Jazz and Blues Bass Line
Spiral Bound ISBN 1-890944-15-7   Perfect Bound ISBN 1890944-16-5

This book covers the basics of bass line construction. A theoretical guide to building bass lines is presented along with 36 chord progressions utilizing the twelve keys of a Major and Minor Blues, plus twelve keys of Rhythm Changes. A reharmonization section is also provided which demonstrates how to reharmonize a chord progression on the spot.

Time Series

The Doing Time series presents a method for contacting, developing and relying on your internal time sense: This series is an excellent source for any musician who is serious about developing strong internal sense of time. This is particularly useful in any kind of music where the rhythms and time signatures may be very complex or free, and there is no conductor.

THE BIG METRONOME
Spiral Bound ISBN 1-890944-37-8   Perfect Bound ISBN 1890944-82-3

The Big Metronome is designed to help you develop a better internal sense of time. This is accomplished by requiring you to "feel time" rather than having you rely on the steady click of a metronome. The idea is to slowly wean yourself away from an external device and rely on your internal/natural sense of time. The exercises presented work in conjunction with the three CDs that accompany this book. CD 1 presents the first 13 settings from a traditional metronome 40-66; the second CD contains metronome markings 69-116, and the third CD contains metronome markings 120-208. The first CD gives you a 2 bar count off and a click every measure, the second CD gives you a 2 bar count off and a click every 2 measures, the 3rd CD gives you a 2 bar count off and a click every 4 measures. By presenting all common metronome markings a student can use these 3 CDs as a replacement for a traditional metronome.

Doing Time with the Blues Volume One:
Spiral Bound ISBN 1-890944-17-3   Perfect Bound ISBN 1890944-78-5

The book and CD presents a method for gaining an internal sense of time thereby eliminating dependence on a metronome. The book presents the basic concept for developing good time and also includes exercises that can be practiced with the CD. The CD provides eight 8 minute tracks at different tempos in which the time is delineated every 2 bars, and with an extra hit every 12 bars to outline the blues form. The student may then use the exercises presented in the book to gain control of their execution or improvise to gain control of their ideas using this bare minimum of time delineation.

Doing Time with the Blues Volume Two:
Spiral Bound ISBN 1-890944-18-1   Perfect Bound ISBN 1890944-79-3

This is the 2nd volume of a four volume series which presents a method for developing a musician's internal sense of time, thereby eliminating dependence on a metronome. This 2nd volume presents different exercises which further the development of this time sense. This 2nd volume begins to test even a professional level player's ability. The CD provides eight 8 minute tracks at different tempos in which the time is delineated every 4 bars with an extra hit every 12 bars to outline the blues form. New exercises are also included that can be practiced with the CD. This series is an excellent source for any musician who is serious about developing an internal sense of time.

Doing Time with 32 bars Volume One:
Spiral Bound ISBN 1-890944-22-X   Perfect Bound ISBN Spiral Bound ISBN 1890944-80-7

The book and CD presents a method for gaining an internal sense of time thereby eliminating dependence on a metronome. The book presents the basic concept for developing good time and also includes exercises that can be practiced with the CD. The CD provides eight 8 minute tracks at different tempos in which the time is delineated every 2 bars, with an extra hit every 32 to outline the 32 bar form. The student may then use the exercises presented in the book to gain control of their execution or improvise to gain control of their ideas using this bare minimum of time delineation.

Doing Time with 32 bars Volume Two:
Spiral Bound ISBN 1-890944-23-8   Perfect Bound ISBN Spiral Bound ISBN 1890944-81-5

This is the 2nd volume of a four volume series which presents a method for developing a musician's internal sense of time, thereby eliminating dependence on a metronome.. This 2nd volume presents different exercises which further the development of this time sense. This 2nd volume begins to test even a professional level player's ability. The CD provides eight 8 minute tracks at different tempos in which the time is delineated every 4 bars with an extra hit every 32 bars to outline the 32 bar form.   New exercises are also included that can be practiced with the CD. This series is an excellent source for any musician who is serious about developing an internal sense of time.

Other Workbooks

Music Theory Workbook for All Instruments, Volume 1: Interval and Chord Construction
Spiral Bound ISBN 1594899-51-7   Perfect Bound ISBN 1890944-46-7

This book provides real hands-on application of intervals and chords. A theory section written in concise and easy to understand language prepares the student for all exercises. Worksheets are given that quiz a student about intervals and chord construction using staff notation. Answers are supplied in the back of the book enabling a student to work without a teacher.

Jazz Piano Vocabulary by Roberta Piket, Volume 1: The Major Scale
Spiral Bound ISBN 1594899-51-7   Perfect Bound ISBN 1594899-52-5

This book is the 1st volume in a series designed to help the student of jazz piano learn and apply jazz scales by mastering each scale and its uses in improvisation. Each book focuses on a different scale, illustrating the scale in all twelve keys with complete fingerings. Also provided are chords and left hand voicings to match, exercises and etudes to apply the material to improvising, ideas for further study and listening, and detailed suggestions on how to practice the material. Volume 1 also includes a detailed primer on note reading, basic theory and rhythmic notation.

Jazz Piano Vocabulary by Roberta Piket, Volume 2: The Dorian Mode
Spiral Bound ISBN 1890944-96-3   Perfect Bound ISDN 1090944-98-X

The 2nd volume in the series, this book focuses on the Dorian scale and applies it to improvising on minor seventh chords. The Dorian scale is presented in all twelve keys with complete fingerings. The book also contains left hand voicings, exercises, many examples, an etude to help apply the material, ideas for further study, an extended discography, and detailed instructions and practice tips.

Jazz Piano Vocabulary by Roberta Piket, Volume 5: The Mixolydian Mode
Spiral Bound ISBN   Perfect Bound ISBN

This book focuses on the Mixolydian scale and applies it to improvising on dominant seventh and dominant seventh sus chords. The scale is presented in all twelve keys with fingerings. The book also contains an introduction to approach notes, an explanation and etude on twelve bar blues form, left hand voicings, exercises, melodic examples, instructions and practice tips.

E-Books

The Bruce Arnold series of instructional E-books is for the student who wishes to target specific areas of study that are of particular interest. Many of these books are excerpted from other larger texts. The excerpted source is listed for each book. These books are available on-line at www.muse-eek.com as well as at many e-tailers throughout the internet. These books can also be purchased in the traditional book binding format. (See the ISBN number for proper format)

Chord Velocity: Volume One, Learning to switch between chords quickly
E-book ISBN 1-890944-88-2

The first hurdle a beginning guitarist encounters is difficulty in switching between chords quickly enough to make a chord progression sound like music. This book provides exercises that help a student gradually increase the speed with which they change chords. Special free audio files are also available on the muse-eek.com website to make practice more productive and fun. With a few weeks, remarkable improvement by can be achieved using this method. This book is excerpted from "1st Steps for a Beginning Guitarist Volume One."

Guitar Technique: Volume One, Learning the basics to fast, clean, accurate and fluid performance skills.
E-book ISBN 1-890944-91-2

This book is for both the beginning guitarist or the more experienced guitarist who wishes to improve their technique. All aspects of the physical act of playing the guitar are covered, from how to hold a guitar to the specific way each hand is involved in the playing process. Pictures and videos are provided to help clarify each technique. These pictures and videos are either contained in the book or can be downloaded at www.muse-eek.com This book is excerpted from "1st Steps for a Beginning Guitarist Volume One."

Accompaniment: Volume One, Learning to Play Bass and Chords Simultaneously
E-book ISBN 1-890944-87-4

The techniques found within this book are an excellent resource for creating and understanding how to play bass and chords simultaneously in a jazz or blues style. Special attention is paid to understanding how this technique is created, thereby enabling the student to recreate this style with other pieces of music. This book is excerpted from the book "Guitar Clinic."

Beginning Rhythm Studies: Volume One, Learning the basics of reading rhythm and playing in time.
E-book ISBN 1-890944-89-0

This book covers the basics for anyone wishing to understand or improve their rhythmic abilities. Simple language is used to show the student how to read and play rhythm. Exercises are presented which can accelerate the learning process. Audio examples in the form of midifiles are available on the muse-eek.com website to facilitate learning the correct rhythm in time. This book is excerpted from the book "Rhythm Primer."